Moral Education in a Secular Society

Moral Education
in a Secular Society

Paul H. Hirst

 University of London Press Ltd
National Children's Home

University of London Press Ltd
St Paul's House, Warwick Lane, London EC4P 4AH

Printed in Great Britain by
NCH Printing Department, Harpenden, Herts.

Bound by Hunter and Foulis Ltd, Edinburgh

Contents

Preface

In agreeing to give the 1974 Convocation Address for the National Children's Home on the subject of moral education in a secular society, I recognised that I should be forced to come off the academic fence on many controversial issues. Producing this much-expanded version of that lecture has given me opportunity to work out in more detail some of my theoretical and practical conclusions, though I am not altogether happy with either the position here outlined or its justification. That morality can no longer be viewed as necessarily dependent on religion seems to me clear on both philosophical and pragmatic grounds. But if that is so, the question then is: on what is the moral life to be based? Only with some answer to that can we begin to outline what the aims of moral education ought now to be. I have tried to tackle these issues at a fairly fundamental level, without presupposing that the reader has any technical philosophical knowledge. Questions of moral education pervade the whole of education, and that not only in schools. Parents and house-parents, as well as teachers, are involved in the business whether they like it or not, and many of the issues I have discussed are therefore of very general significance. Though certain parts of this volume are not easy reading and others are directed primarily to teachers, I hope the treatment is such that it will be of interest to a wide audience of both professional and non-professional educators.

I am grateful to those who persuaded me to undergo the discipline of producing this introductory text. My thanks are due to the Reverend Gordon Barritt, Principal of the National Children's Home, for all his help and consideration when I was heavily pressed by other commitments whilst writing this volume. To my secretary, Miss Valerie Horler, I am also much indebted. Above all, however, I owe a debt of gratitude to those many authors, some of them close friends, from whom I have learnt so much. It is impossible in a work of this kind to acknowledge their influence fully, though the major writings on which I have drawn are referred to in the references. To Professor Richard Peters I clearly owe a very particular debt. It is largely as a result of listening to him and reading his writings that I have managed to find my way at all within the maze of problems that moral education raises. The use to which I have put many of his ideas is, however, my own and I have at times only partially, and no doubt inaccurately, expressed what he has had to say. I would therefore urge on all those who read this volume a study of his very considerable contribution to our understanding of this area of education.

Paul H. Hirst

Cambridge, June 1974

CHAPTER I

Secularisation and the Problem of Moral Education

Secularisation has taken many forms, and can be seen in many aspects of human life. Yet all the changes involved are linked together by one common feature: a decay in the use of religious concepts and beliefs.[1] This is not, of course, to imply that there ever was a time or a society in which all men used such concepts, or that those who used them agreed in their religious beliefs. Nor is it to deny that religious matters remain of central concern to some. What it means, however, is that there was a time when more people were intellectually and emotionally involved in religious concerns and often to a much greater degree than is now the case, and that social and institutional relations were formerly viewed in religious terms that are now only very rarely voiced. The causes of these changes are in detail a matter of dispute, but it is widely agreed that certain interlocking social and intellectual developments are at the heart of the matter. Intellectually, the rise of science has undoubtedly been crucial and it is tempting to see this as the simple key to the whole process. With the seeming unending growth of scientific understanding, religious understanding has progressively come to look more and more redundant. With a decline in specifically religious beliefs, social and institutional relations have come to be viewed in a new secular light. On this account, intellectual changes result in social changes. Such an approach is, however, too simple, for intellectual changes are often, indeed some have argued always, the product not the cause of social and economic changes. Has not the growth of urbanisation itself been a cause of the decay in religious beliefs? Is it not true that the pattern of life in a modern city is what makes religious belief seem irrelevant for most people? But then again, can one not argue that if urban society itself changes the pattern of thought for most of us, that society would not have come about without the development of scientific technology? Clearly, social and intellectual changes operate on each other in complex ways and at different levels.[2]

But though elucidating the causes of secularisation may be extremely difficult, a description of the major changes it has involved in our own society may not be so hard a task. Intellectually, the decay of religious concepts has meant that supernatural interpretations of experience have been progressively replaced by others. That is not to say that secularisation leaves us with a totally materialistic view of the universe and that the only form of understanding that is acceptable is to be found in the sciences. That is only one very particular and perhaps extreme form of secular thought. The loss of religious categories must not be thought to entail the loss as well of all other non-scientific categories, say the aesthetic, mental, moral and metaphysical. What it does mean is that science and all these other categories are regarded as functioning in their own right, independently of any religious considerations, and having a status that means religious considerations can be ignored. To areas of secular thought, all religious thought or determination is irrelevant. It is not a necessary part of such areas that all religious beliefs can be shown to be unintelligible or false. It is rather that the latter come to be seen as of no consequence, having nothing to contribute in our efforts to understand ourselves and our world and to determine how we are to live. In the case of the totally secular mind, religious concepts and beliefs are either unintelligible, inconsistent with secular thought, or false. But such a secularist might well share many other areas of concepts and beliefs with those who do subscribe to a religious position. Where there is this overlap, either the secularist and the religious believer must share some non-religious basis for their beliefs, or they must be willing to agree about these beliefs whilst differing about their justification. Many who deny the meaningfulness of Christian claims share with Christians not only vast areas of scientific understanding but also moral and social ideals. The overlap in their ideas of the justification for scientific claims may be complete; in the areas of moral and social ideas it may well be much less. Clearly, there are possible many positions in which a measure of secular thought is accepted, yet a degree of significance for religious beliefs is insisted on. Many Christians accept, for instance, the secular character of the sciences, but reject a similar account of moral understanding. What is of particular importance, however, is that there are nowadays not lacking Christians who seek to go along with the total secularist to the full in all non-religious areas, whilst maintaining that religious beliefs are not thereby rendered unintelligible or illusory. Rather, such secular Christians, as I shall call them, would claim that the true character of their religious beliefs only emerges when they are combined with a thorough secularisation of all other areas of human thought and experience. On this view religious beliefs, rightly understood, are not a proper basis for scientific, moral, aesthetic, or other beliefs; rather they complement these other forms of belief in some way and are even perhaps in significant measure dependent on them. In this complex situation it is perhaps wise to think of the intellectual areas of secularisation as, in the first instance, the development of the sciences, morals, art, social and political thought as autonomous areas. How far such secularisation is reconcilable with religious beliefs can then be regarded as a further question to which there are a number of different answers, dependent on the particular religious beliefs under consideration and how they are in fact to be construed.

The development of secularisation viewed in these terms must inevitably mean that, where religious beliefs and practices are maintained, they are progressively 'privatised'. The more secular society becomes, the more its social life and institutions become determined by considerations that are acceptable to all, no matter what their attitude to religious beliefs. In so far as religious and non-religious people can agree about social principles, religious questions can be regarded as a private, personal matter. In so far as people can also agree on a secular basis on which to settle matters of disagreement about social issues, the more firmly privatised religious concerns become. Such firm privatisation is increasingly the mark of our own secular society, in which the widest range of attitudes to religious beliefs is acceptable, provided they are never allowed to determine public issues. Public life and public institutions are thus becoming totally profane, though some public display of religion may remain. At best, this can be seen as a way of affirming shared values previously associated with religion, if now held by many independently of that. Expressed another way, it is a mark of the secular society that it is religiously pluralist, tolerating all forms of religious belief and practice that do not contravene agreed public principles. Such tolerance and pluralism mean that a diversity of personal life styles is possible within a common framework. What it also seems to mean in practice is that public issues are approached pragmatically with the aim of finding agreed answers to particular issues without looking further than is absolutely necessary into individual purposes and ideals. What will work in a context of very varied ultimate beliefs tends to dominate the scene rather than any more fundamental consideration of what is ultimately more defensible. There is a tendency, too, for the acceptance of a pluralism of personal private beliefs to lead to an easy assumption of relativism—that all beliefs in this area are equally justifiable, being matters of personal choice and decision. What is more, this tendency carries over very readily to the belief that, even in matters of agreed public principle, there is no ultimate justification and our common acceptance of a principle is a decision purely relative to our present time and place. [3]

But these patterns of thought that are characteristic of secularisation have to be seen alongside the patterns of social and institutional life in which they are, at least in our society, commonly expressed and without which, as was said earlier, they might not even have come to exist. Modern urban life encapsulates the secular society. In it individuals play a minute part within a vast social system, their public functions in society being limited and specialised. Few if any understand in any depth the intricate pattern of the over-all relationships between these functions and many have little or no grasp of the wider significance of many of the roles they play. Relations within functional groups are to a high degree depersonalised, the groups existing for particular restricted ends. To survive, let alone succeed, in this situation demands above all a pragmatic approach. Working the system in its varied parts is essential, and keeping it working by one's own contribution is what is demanded. Provided one is able to use the opportunities within the system, the possibilities it offers are vast and varied. At the same time, the fragmentation, specialisation and bureaucratisation in the system make it immensely difficult for many to gain access to those opportunities. Choice and variety are of the essence of urban life, but at the price of functional relationships and a complex system in which many individuals find themselves unable to get access to what is certainly available to others. The life of the individual in such a society is largely characterised by the particular selection of functions and roles which he fulfils, only some of which will be of his personal choice. Though this selection may have some personal stamp, within most of these functions the individual is simply marked by his carrying out the role. He is an anonymous participant. Personal relationships of any significance are by the nature of the case progressively excluded from a pattern of life increasingly composed in this way, and it is therefore not surprising that in urban society people jealously guard those areas of privacy that are left. The multiplicity of limited relationships urban life demands are such that their anonymity must be accepted. To seek to make them personal is indeed to run counter to their necessary character and, what is more to the point, recognising their anonymity is the very means for preserving even a limited number of relationships at a personal level.

As the specialised roles in urban life are essentially pragmatic in character, focusing on the attainment of limited ends, there is in general no place in them for religious considerations; they are essentially secular. Religion is then a matter for the private area of personal life which impinges on the public life of society only through the selection of functions and roles which individuals take on. Institutionally, of course, the churches themselves tend to become functionalised on the secular model, operating a pragmatic system concerned to offer certain specialised 'products' for members of the society who happen to want them. But these institutions nowadays simply exist alongside many others which provide optional extras. They are peripheral to the system as a whole and totally irrelevant when it comes to the working of the public system in everyday life. Just as in intellectual affairs religious thought has been displaced by the growth of autonomous, secular areas of thought, so in society religious institutions have been displaced by the growth of autonomous, secular institutions.[4]

These general comments on the secularity of modern urban life do not, of course, begin to exhaust its characteristics, and that was not the intention behind them. Nothing explicit has been said, for instance, about the sheer density of population, modern means of transport and communication, insulation from the natural world and its rhythms. These and many other features are of great importance in modern life and no doubt they have been highly significant in the development of secularity. It is the distinctive character of secularity itself that has concerned me, because it is the significance of this particular feature of our intellectual and social life for moral education that I want to explore. In a society that sees itself as subscribing to a common religion and in which strong religious institutions are centrally important, morality derives its intellectual and social character and force from that religion. The ultimacy of religious considerations means that, in so far as these have a moral import, they are to the religious adherent the ultimate authority. Moral education in such a context is necessarily seen as interlocked with religious education. But what about a secular society?

If it is a fact that in our own society religious institutions of all kinds are of central social significance no longer, if intellectually many find religious concepts and beliefs unintelligible or irrelevant, if for those who retain religious beliefs and practices these are now effectively reduced to being a private and personal matter whether they like it or not, what is now to be done about moral education? To answer that question first demands clarity about how in our present intellectual and social context we conceive morality. It demands an examination of the foundations of morality both intellectually and in practice. It demands an examination of the relevant processes of education. This is a tall order. On many crucial relevant matters there is great diversity of opinion. On many others our sheer ignorance of the facts is immense. It is difficult for one author to begin to do justice to areas of thought in which he is an amateur. What is here offered is therefore just one attempt at an introduction to some of the interrelated issues. It takes a particular stand on certain matters of very real controversy, and it is no doubt in parts ill-considered and ill-informed. To stick one's neck out like this is alien to the academic mind. But educational practice will not wait for measured careful academic conclusions, and moral education is going on for good and ill.

The following chapters seek simply to make some positive contribution to the consideration of what precisely we ought to be doing in our secular context. In the process an attempt is made to see the situation from the point of view of a not inconsiderable number of teachers who, though they recognise that religion is 'privatised', can see no satisfactory anchor for public morality outside religion. If they personally reject all forms of religion, they are uncertain of the basis on which moral education in schools and other institutions can properly be conducted. If they personally accept a particular religious position, there is an inevitable tension between their personal moral convictions and their inability to see an appropriate basis for moral education in public institutions. What we need to discover is whether or not there is indeed a secular form of moral education that is satisfactorily based, and, if so, how far it is compatible with religious beliefs. The approach to moral education that emerges in these pages is undoubtedly secular, but it takes a form that is not inconsistent with certain interpretations of Christian belief. It is hoped therefore that it will prove of interest not only to total secularists but to those who, whilst subscribing to many of the developments of secularism, remain convinced of the importance of religious claims and even perhaps of the truth of certain central tenets of Christianity.

References

1 As this book is concerned primarily with secularisation in our society, the term 'religion' is used throughout with the Christian religion in mind. However, much if not all that is said about religion applies to other faiths as well.
2 See MACINTYRE, A. (1967). *Secularisation and Moral Change*. London: Oxford University Press.
3 I have discussed this and other aspects of 'privatisation' in HIRST, P. H. (1967). Public and Private Values and Religious Educational Content. In Sizer, T. R. (ed.), *Religion and Public Education*. Boston, Mass.: Houghton Mifflin.
   See also BAIER, K. (1971). Ethical Pluralism and Moral Education. In Beck, C. M., Crittenden, B. S., Sullivan, E. V. (eds.). *Moral Education*. Toronto: University of Toronto Press.
4 For a further discussion see:
   COX, H. (1965). *The Secular City*. London: Macmillan.
   CALLAHAN, D. (ed.) (1966). *The Secular City Debate*. London: Macmillan.
   SHEPHERD, D. (1974). *Built as a City*. London: Hodder and Stoughton.

CHAPTER 2

Morality and the Christian Tradition

THE NATURE OF MORAL BELIEFS

It is characteristic of human beings that they hold beliefs about how they themselves and other men ought to live, what they should and should not do, what kind of people they ought or ought not to be. These beliefs about character and conduct, which are often expressed in judgments about what is right and what is wrong, what is good and what is bad, are what in a general sense we mean by moral beliefs. Telling the truth, doing properly the job for which one is paid, causing minimum suffering to others, being courageous, just, unselfish, these are all examples of moral beliefs to which many of us would subscribe.

The moral life of any particular person is not, however, as we all know, a simple matter. Even if the core of it is a body of beliefs, there is the huge question as to which beliefs are to be embraced. And if we can settle that, there is the equally enormous problem of actually in practice living accordingly. Both these issues involve immense complexities. If we take the question of which beliefs are to be accepted, we are first faced with the great diversity of the areas of human life and action to which they must relate, to matters of sex relations, bringing up children, business affairs, national government, gambling, housing, finance, to name but a few. Then there is the problem of the interrelationship of the many different aspects of human actions and the implications that come from this. The level of salary I think appropriate for the job I do may involve my relations with colleagues, the future of my children, my attitude to the Third World and to pensioners, my notions of the role of trade unions, my attitude to the law and so on. There is, too, the question of the generality of the moral beliefs I have. Some may be very specific about particular actions I consider unacceptable, say smoking pot or using my office telephone for personal calls. Others may be much wider beliefs in, say, the desirability of preserving freedom, of showing love and concern, beliefs that in themselves seem to prescribe no particular actions. How are these to be related? And then how exactly is one to justify one's beliefs against any others when manifestly there is such radical disagreement, not only as to what beliefs should be held but even about the way in which one might set about justifying any beliefs at all?

And if we take the question of living according to one's beliefs, the situation is no less complicated. No one's life is or could be simply determined by the direct conscious application of his personal beliefs. What is more, one's moral beliefs can be quite alarmingly inconsistent. What I think parents ought to do for their children can be totally irreconcilable with what in fact I do about my own. There are wants and desires of many kinds that are in no sense the ready servants of intellectual judgments. Long-standing attitudes, moods and emotional responses are elements that act as aids or hindrances in so far as they are or are not harmonised with one's moral beliefs. Equally, many matters of actions are not, and in practice cannot be, deliberated on, so that, if one is to live the moral life, one's beliefs must somehow inform one's habits and unconsciously expressed dispositions. The context in which we live is such that we have many social roles where there are external controls over our actions, sanctions and rewards which we must accept as forms of reality. Often the consequences of these roles and of personal relations in society result in situations in no sense of our choosing or willing. The situation could be elaborated further, but from these considerations alone it surely follows that, even if we could find a set of appropriately justifiable beliefs, there would remain the problem of the mechanisms of the moral life whereby these beliefs come to inform appropriately all that we in fact do.

I am not wanting to suggest that these two enormous questions of 'what beliefs?' and 'how can we live by them?' are totally dissociated. Nor, clearly, do I wish to minimise their complexities. Nevertheless, they are, I think, distinguishable and together they seem to me to raise the most fundamental issues of morality. If we could be clearer on these two scores we might, I think, know where we want to go in moral education. Religious and secular views can differ widely on both what beliefs we should live by and how we can in fact live by them. They can therefore present widely differing educational demands. But not all sets of moral beliefs are equally justifiable, nor are all accounts of the mechanisms of the moral life. I shall therefore take these two areas in turn and seek critically to assess what in our contemporary context we can most reasonably say about them. From these considerations the task of moral education in our secular society will, I hope, become clearer.

Moral beliefs I have so far described very generally as concerned with what men should or should not be or do. If one looks at the beliefs of this kind that men hold, however, some of them are, to say the least, thoroughly trivial, like the belief that a man ought to wear a tie in a public restaurant, or that one ought to serve coffee after dinner. Others are more serious in their import, like the principle of not driving above 30 m.p.h. in towns, or being punctual for one's appointments. Yet others seem very fundamental indeed, like the protection of people from personal injury, the practice of truth telling, or the maintenance of justice. It is in fact only the more fundamental beliefs of this kind that we usually consider to be moral in character and, if we are to get at the foundations of morality, it is important to clear out of the way considerations which are either irrelevant or secondary. This is all the more important as, though morality is rightly taken to be concerned with judgments as to what ought or ought not to be done, what is right or wrong, good or bad, all these words are also used for judgments which are in any strict sense not themselves moral.

To say what ought to be done in a context where one is simply pointing out what is involved in sticking to some existing custom or tradition (as, for example, when saying that one ought to introduce younger people to their elders and not vice versa) is not to say that this action is morally right. Of course, something that is right according to a tradition may also be morally right, but it may not, and the two judgments need to be kept distinct. Matters of custom and tradition are not necessarily morally justified: indeed, as we are nowadays only too aware, custom or tradition of itself morally justifies nothing.

In the same way, to say that something is what ought to be done according to the law of the land is quite distinct from saying it is morally right. Adultery is not contrary to the law, but to many it is nevertheless morally wrong. Matters of what is right or wrong in law are established by decisions in Parliament and case-law. These may or may not coincide with what is held to be morally right or wrong. Indeed, much debate about the law is about whether or not the laws are morally defensible, a type of criticism which presupposes the very difference between legal and moral judgments to which I am drawing attention. Again, political judgments are not to be confused with moral judgments. To say it is politically right to act in a certain way may well be to say no more than that this is the best way of getting what one wants in the circumstances rather than that it is the morally right thing to do. Politics is the art of the possible, as Lord Butler has so forcefully reminded us, though, of course, many a politically right action is also the morally right thing to do. Equally, in individual affairs, to judge what is prudent in looking after one's own interests, irrespective of the concerns of others, is not thereby to make a moral judgment.

Yet again, though this is to anticipate other things I wish to argue later, to say an act is in accordance with a religious principle or belief is not, I think, to say the same thing as that it is morally right. Telling the truth, or loving one's neighbour, most of us do indeed hold to be morally right. That these are also in accordance with divinely revealed principles or the will of God, and in that sense right, may also be the case, though many would dispute the claim. But whether one agrees or not with the religious judgment, that and the moral judgment must surely be kept distinct. Even if one holds that every morally right act is also in accordance with the will of God, and these two judgments or beliefs always go together, they must nevertheless, I think, be distinguished if we are not to assume from the start the highly debatable claim that what is morally right is necessarily a matter of religious belief.

Finally, I think we must distinguish beliefs as to what morally ought to be done from beliefs as to what ought to be done as a means to some predetermined end. The true belief that if one wants hot water for a bath one ought to turn on the immersion heater is not a moral belief. Nor is the belief that if one wants to keep healthy one ought to have a balanced diet. Keeping healthy may be itself a moral duty, but that one ought to have a balanced diet to achieve that is simply a matter of empirical or scientific fact.

To any one of these distinctions, perhaps particularly that between moral and religious judgments, you may wish to object. What each of these distinctive uses of terms like 'right', 'ought', or 'good' does, you may wish to argue, is to lay down a particular form of morality. To some people these judgments just are religious judgments and that is their morality. To others they just are prudential and that is their morality. Certainly I do not wish to deny for a moment that some people live entirely by religious or prudential claims and employ these terms in that way only. What I might then seem to be doing is to advocate another particular form of morality whose character is as yet only partially disclosed. In one sense this reply is perfectly acceptable to me, for I am indeed concerned with a particular set of rules or principles that can characterise a person's life. But that this is just another alternative morality I would not accept. It seems to me that thoughtful people now, as always, have been concerned that, whatever principles of life and conduct they embrace, they shall be those for which we have maximum justification. We really do seek an answer to the question: why these rules and principles and not some others? Thoughtful people have therefore always used terms like right, ought, and good, not only when referring to matters like law and custom, where it can be seen that the rules do not rest on an ultimately adequate base and thus need further justification, but also to pick out those principles they think ultimately defensible. What I am calling the moral use of these terms is thus an outcome of recognising the ultimate inadequacy of living according to law, or custom, say. If I am taken therefore to be characterising a rational 'morality', as distinct from a prudential, traditional or religious 'morality', I do not mind, for to seek a justifiable and defensible morality is to seek a rational morality. What matters is whether or not I am right that these and other 'moralities', which to my mind are not worthy of that label, are ultimately unacceptable in the basis for principles of conduct that they provide. That custom, law, political and prudential claims are of themselves not ultimate when we seek for justification surely needs little further argument. That religious rules and principles do not of themselves have an adequate justification I shall shortly discuss more explicitly. At this point I simply wish to suggest that it is distinctive of moral discourse that it is concerned with judgments that are ultimate, and defensibly so on rational grounds.[1]

ASPECTS OF THE MORAL LIFE

These distinctions lead to the conclusion that moral beliefs are about what is good or right in human actions and activities in an ultimate sense that overrides all other considerations. Such beliefs in fact express the ultimate values of life in terms of which all other things are judged. Having said that, however, it is surely important for us to go on to discover the ways in which we generally mark out these ultimate values and how we seek from them to judge the worth of the vast range of human pursuits. Above all, we express both what is morally right or wrong in matters of obligation, and good or bad in matters of worthwhile pursuits, in certain explicit rules or principles. Sometimes these refer to particular actions or activities, like killing others, sexual relations, promise-keeping, playing games, or the study of history, which are said to be right, wrong, good, or bad. Sometimes they refer to more general characteristics of actions or activities, for instance that they are unjust, show consideration for the interests of others, or are concerned with the pursuit of truth. Secondly, moral beliefs are also often expressed in terms of virtues or vices, personal qualities like honesty, generosity or cowardliness, which pick out a person's dispositions to live according to certain rules or principles. Like rules and principles they can be at different levels, qualities like integrity, autonomy, or wisdom being complex high-level characteristics that presuppose many lower-level qualities organised into a distinctive pattern. Though traits of these kinds may not be so seen, they are sometimes consciously set out as ideals for the moral life and thus become themselves the objects of moral beliefs. Virtues and vices, however, can only be distinguished in the last analysis by the kinds of action and activities in which they are expressed. Their moral character is therefore in the end determined by the rules or principles of behaviour which they embody in complex dispositional form. A similar view must, I think, be taken of the motives which we often consider lie behind human actions and activities. Pride, ambition, or love, for example, can be seen as motives of which we may or may not be aware, and as such are dispositions to act or believe which involve morally significant rules and principles.

The terms we use for motives are, however, also frequently used for patterns of emotional response which may or may not accompany the disposition. This raises the question of the moral significance of emotions, the third area of human life in which there is a moral element. In emotional responses we can, I think, only distinguish this moral element by once more looking at the rules or principles of conduct that are implicit. It is now widely accepted that all emotions, at least in adult life, are tied to particular self-referring beliefs about a situation. I feel proud, for example, when I think myself responsible for something which others respect or admire. But these beliefs can include beliefs of a moral kind, as when in remorse I judge myself responsible for a wrong action. If this is so, then it is these beliefs that would seem to determine the immediate moral character of the emotions, the affective occurrences themselves being of secondary importance. That I feel remorse is significant morally in that it implies that I believe I have done wrong. But that belief may in fact be at odds with what I intellectually hold. Emotions are thus an important factor in indicating the moral beliefs to which I am disposed on certain matters affecting me. The pleasure or pain of the emotion which underscores my beliefs can also itself provide a reason for doing or refraining from doing what I believe to be right or wrong. It remains, however, true that it is in terms of the moral rules or principles they embody that emotions come to have any moral character they possess. They voice conscious or unconscious moral beliefs. Of course, in so far as the emotions a person experiences result in mental disturbances and behaviour that interfere with his understanding and action, they can become the objects of moral appraisal like all other traits because of the behaviour in which they result, even if the person concerned cannot be held responsible for such behaviour on the occasion.

Mention must finally be made of a fourth way in which moral judgments are expressed: in our concepts of the social roles that we are all involved in. In any complex society, patterns of expected behaviour and character are built into the social structure. Even in a society in which diverse styles of life are possible, the role of parent, for example, has certain moral principles associated with it. Many professional roles, for instance those of doctor and lawyer, have explicitly expressed professional codes of behaviour associated with them, but even the most routine and mechanical jobs are not without their moral demands in terms of, say, honesty and conscientiousness. With these roles usually go many social sanctions, some of these being embodied in a formal legal structure. Complex though the moral content of such roles and institutional practices may be, they do not, I think, introduce any fundamentally new elements which must be built into our understanding of moral judgments.[2]

In recognising that morality is expressed in these many different aspects of life, we can, I think, see the unsatisfactoriness of any loose characterisation of it in terms which do not make the underlying rules and principles clear. The tendency to think of the moral life under one simple term, as, say, the life of love, is particularly unhelpful. To begin with, such a term is ambiguous, for it can label an emotion or feeling, a disposition to act in certain ways, a set of principles, accepting certain social roles, perhaps some, all, or even none of these things. If it is taken as labelling romantic passion, its moral character will be based on implicit principles of one distinctive sort. If it is taken as the principle that one ought to seek the unlimited good of others, the resulting actions may be very different. But in either case, if we are to be able to form any accurate idea of what is being said, we need a much fuller statement of the rules and principles the person expresses. To approve morally of romantic passion is in the end dependent on approving its outcomes in action, and we cannot judge that without being able to distinguish these from other actions. If love is defined as seeking the good of others, that of itself tells us nothing. We need to know what exactly this person considers the good of others to be. Love is a general term that can be used to cover many different types of actions, and only if we know which can we understand the morality concerned.[3] It therefore seems to me that whatever other forms of moral expression there are in the moral life, be they actions, dispositions, emotions, or roles, we can only distinguish their moral significance for what it is in terms of the rules or principles for conduct which they enshrine. It is actions and activities that ultimately have moral value and all other aspects of the moral life have their value in relation to those. In seeking to understand the basis of moral claims then, and in trying to answer the question as to what morality we ought to pursue, it is the basis of these rules and principles we must sort out.

But ultimate rules and principles of conduct can be, as was pointed out earlier, of many different levels, some dealing with specific actions like theft, others dealing with general issues like the maximisation of freedom. How then are we to think of these? Do they form a disparate set of isolated rules, or ought they to be thought of as part of a coherent system of some sort? Of course, as a matter of fact the rules and principles that govern the lives of many people may be disparate and often inconsistent. The very complexities of the personal aspects of the moral life, and the great diversity of the many-faceted situations with which we are called to deal, mean that few if any of us are likely, in practice, to be totally consistent. Nevertheless, to have a morality at all is to have certain rules or principles considered ultimate, and that alone is to be committed to at least seeking for some order and consistency in one's pattern of life. The question that must first be looked at is therefore how far the pursuit of coherence of the principles themselves is possible, irrespective of our living by them. Moreover, if we are concerned, as I am presuming we are, about having justification for the rules and principles by which we live, we are on that score also concerned with exploring whatever consistency and coherence is possible in this area. A justifiable morality is necessarily one that has a structure uniting seemingly disparate elements by virtue of the justificatory procedure.

THE MARKS OF MORAL REASONING

If, following this line of approach, we look at all closely at the arguments by which we seek to solve moral dilemmas, we discover that attempts to reason out what ought to be done have a number of specific features that illuminate the character of moral rules in any rational morality.

First, as in all other areas of reasoning, we seek to understand particular situations in terms of the general rules or principles that apply in this situation. Why does this particular substance expand when it is heated? Because it is a metal and all metals expand when heated. Why ought I to meet Mr X at 10 a.m.? Because I promised to meet him then and I ought to keep my promises. It is general rules that justify our particular actions.

Secondly, if we then go on to ask why we should accept the general rules we invoke, we often seek the answer to this by appeal to yet more general rules which are held to justify the more specific ones. A teacher ought to mark a pupil's essay because he ought to mark all essays he has asked for in his teaching. Why that? Because he ought to carry out the duties for which he is employed. Why that? Because he ought to keep the obligations he undertook when accepting the post. Why that? Clearly, this chain of reasoning must stop somewhere, and where exactly is crucial as we shall see, but at present I am merely pointing out that moral reasoning takes this form of justification by appeal to more fundamental principles.

But thirdly, in many cases moral issues are too complex to be dealt with under one particular rule or chain of rules. The question as to what I ought to do with my time on a Saturday may involve a number of conflicting claims. There is, say, the duty to an elderly parent who is dependent on me for comfort, reassurance and advice. There is the question of those household repairs that I cannot really afford to get someone else to do. There is my duty to my children who need parental interest and care whilst my wife needs a rest from these demands. There is, say, my duty to my research as well as my own need for peace and relaxation. Each of these claims on my time may well be justifiable by some appropriate chain of argument. Philosophers specialise in producing rather artificial examples that can bring out conflicts of this kind, such as the case of the homicidal maniac who arrives at the door asking where to find someone who is in fact in the house. What in this case about the principle of telling the truth, which here conflicts with the principle of minimising suffering? A person sophisticated in moral considerations, however, will recognise that these conflicts of moral rules or principles, which arise when they are applied in particular cases, is of the very nature of decisions about human action. Our actions have many facets and many implications which vary according to differences in context. What moral rules can do is pick out one, or at most a limited pattern, of the facets and say what is right or wrong, good or bad, in that connection only. To say that taking another's property, so causing unnecessary suffering, is wrong is to say that in so far as actions have these stated characteristics, they are wrong. But in so far as they have certain other characteristics, they might in those respects be right. In the technical jargon, moral principles must be seen as having a prima facie character; in so far as other things are not considered or are considered equal, taking these aspects alone, this is the moral rule. That we shall not infrequently come across a conflict of rules or principles is therefore but a consequence of their necessarily limited nature.[4] Of course, particular moral theories have sometimes sought to suggest that one particular ultimate principle might resolve conflicts between other moral principles, but these theories have usually had the effect of submerging the problem of conflict under some elusive and not readily defensible notion. The complexity of human actions would suggest that so convenient an answer to our dilemmas is not likely to be readily forthcoming.

If these three characteristics of moral rules and principles are accepted, that particular actions or activities are justified by appeal to general rules, that their justification is in turn by appeal to yet more general principles, and that they are necessarily partial in their application, which means that moral dilemmas may not be uniquely decidable even in the ultimate, the answer to the question as to which morality we ought to have is a matter of discovering which principles of conduct have the most adequate justification when we argue back to the most fundamental principles of all. Men have given very different accounts of what those ultimately justifiable principles are, just as they have given very different accounts as to how that justification is possible. Not surprisingly, some have argued that fundamental principles, just because they are fundamental, cannot be

justified. In that case, perhaps they are necessarily matters of decision
when at best we can know what they will entail and thus discover
what we prefer, there being no ultimate reason for that preference.
Or perhaps they must be matters of faith or commitment to an
authority or source that is superior to human reason. To this million
dollar question and the validity of secularised approaches to it I
must now turn.

THE CHRISTIAN TRADITION AND MORAL RULES

It would be seriously misleading to suggest that there is any one
detailed account of the justification of fundamental moral principles
that has ever been generally accepted by Christians. Within both
Protestant and Catholic traditions, however, there are two long-
standing patterns of general approach which have influenced most
popular ideas of the bases of Christian morality and it is these two
approaches that have been increasingly called in question with the
growth of secularisation.

In the first of these, the rules and principles of conduct that
characterise the moral life are seen as indissolubly, even logically,
tied into a much wider system of religious beliefs. That wider system
can therefore be regarded as providing the justification for the moral
rules and principles within it. How this appeal is made in detail
varies in Christian thought. In general the rules and principles are
seen as justified because they have been given in an authoritative
revelation in Scripture, in the person of Jesus Christ, by grace through
the Church, or by grace to the individual mind perhaps through the
operation of conscience. One of these sources may be seen as central,
providing the beliefs which set the norms for judging claims from the
other sources. A combination of certain of these sources may be seen
as providing a complex pattern of corroborating checks, coherence
and consistency being regarded as necessary marks of valid moral
claims. However, it has to be accepted that if certain moral beliefs
are to be justified, to know their source does not of itself give us a
justification for the moral pronouncements. Any adequate justification of moral beliefs along these lines must justify one accepting as
ultimate what comes from this source and from no other. But how is
that to be done? In answer, Christian thinkers have usually sought
to argue that the justification comes from the source of the beliefs
being an omnipotent, omniscient creator who thereby knows what is

right and good for man. But there are vast difficulties in such an account. Even if it could be shown that there exists a being with these attributes and that we could know which expressions of a moral kind come from him, both immensely difficult claims, there is a need to know that what is said is indeed right and good, for an omnipotent, omniscient creator cannot be assumed to be good. Indeed, there might be thought to be plenty of evidence to the contrary. But if we must know that this omnipotent, omniscient creator is also good before we are justified in accepting what he reveals, on what grounds can we claim to know that, when we are trying to maintain that our knowledge of what is good comes only from what this being reveals? We can have no grounds for accepting what he says until we know that he is good, but we cannot know that he is good other than by accepting what he says. Put another way, this point is simply an extension of a point I made earlier when talking of moral issues being overriding. For something to be announced by an authority of some sort, legal, traditional, or, as in this case, religious, does not make it a moral rule. The moral status of a rule announced by an authority is dependent on its having moral justification, not power, status, or even omniscience and omnipotence behind it. If we are to have a moral justification for accepting a moral authority, that authority cannot itself provide the foundation of our moral beliefs.

Certain Christian thinkers have endeavoured to reply to this difficulty by arguing that no further justification for what is revealed, beyond knowing that it is revealed by an omnipotent, omniscient creator, is necessary because what he reveals defines what is good and right. This is a rather desperate solution, however. What it does is redefine the terms in a way that only masks a genuine difficulty. For why, after all, should we do what is expressed by such a being even if that is what we will now call good and right? What is now being offered is a very particular form of morality and one in which the moral life is reduced to a form of obedience with no further justification. Such justification is ruled out of court by a trick of definition. This is a particular form of morality which many of us would reject as abhorrent because of its arbitrariness. There seems to me to be no escape from the conclusion that the claim that the ultimate justification for moral beliefs lies simply in revelation of some sort is untenable, even granted that we could justify the claim that an omnipotent, omniscient creator exists and that we could identify his revelations. For, granted all that, we would at best know what that being rules or wills and that is not of itself to have a foundation to morality.

Yet this appeal to revelation as the ultimate basis of a justifiable morality is enormously attractive to Christians and it is perhaps important that we try to discover why. I suggest the attraction lies in a deep confusion between a belief central to all traditional forms of Christianity and the untenable thesis I have been discussing. It is one thing to argue that God is the source of all moral rules because he is the ultimate creator of all things and those rules are the expression of his will; it is quite another to say that the ultimate justification for our moral rules is that he is their source. To seek a justification is to look for proper defence of those rules that warrants our believing them, and a story of the origin of them, even if it is complemented by a story of the origins of our need for justification and of the procedures of justification, does not itself provide the justification.

The same distinction holds in all other areas of human understanding. To believe that Newton's Laws of Motion have their origins in the will of God is one thing. For us to have proper grounds for believing Newton's Laws to be true is another matter. Even if Newton had formulated those Laws from a study of Scripture, or after communion with God in prayer, their justification would remain a matter of experimental investigation. Indeed, we would be likely to accept their source as being from God, that the communication is in fact a revelation, only when we had proper justification for them. What Newton's Laws state is that physical bodies behave in certain ways; whether we are justified in believing that they do can only be properly determined by seeing if they do. The very meaning of the terms in which the Laws are expressed lays down how they can be known to be true. For these Laws to be reported or announced to us by any source, however ultimate it is as a source, does not change the grounds on which we are ultimately justified in believing them. A revelation of Newton's Laws could only be properly regarded as justifying them if we already knew that the source had itself proper means of justifying them. For us to know that means, we must ourselves have the means of checking. True, if a source is repeatedly checked and produces justified beliefs, we may then have grounds for accepting certain beliefs we have not checked. But if we have no means of checking any beliefs of this kind, only their assertion by some source, we have no justification for them in the end. Belief that God is the source of certain beliefs does not itself provide us with justification for believing them to be true, unless we know that source to be a proper source for such truths, and that demands that we can already judge truths in this area ourselves. Justification is something we must seek in our human situation, for without that, belief and conduct are in the end arbitrary. Many religious claims may be true and many moral truths may have been expressed in revelation. But whatever is claimed, however attractive or internally consistent, it cannot properly be accepted by us unless there is justification for believing it to be true and justification appropriate to the character of the belief.

Expressed more technically, the point is that we must distinguish between metaphysical and epistemological issues. Morality or science may or may not be rooted in God's existence and nature. That is a metaphysical question. But even if it is so rooted, it does not follow that a knowledge of God's existence and nature is necessary to our knowledge of moral or scientific rules and principles. The epistemological question of the basis of our knowledge of such principles is another matter, and in each case that basis must always be appropriate to the kind of knowledge that is being pursued. Morality is not being made prior to God or placed above him. It is simply that our knowledge of morality is logically prior to our knowledge of God, and that our claims to know about the moral nature of God depend on our having autonomously based moral knowledge. In moral matters that means an argument that sticks to the point that it is justification that is needed and not something else, that does not beg the question, and that does not sidestep the issue by falsely trying to justify moral matters on non-moral grounds.[5]

The second long-standing approach within Christian ethics to the justification of fundamental moral principles runs into none of the difficulties of the first. Though God is acknowledged as the ultimate source of all, including all moral principles, our knowledge of them, including the justification we can have for them, is seen as something which we can at least in part have independently of any particular revelation. Moral truths may well be revealed by God in many ways, but we are able genuinely to recognise their moral excellence by means of a prior grasp of moral principles that we have by nature or reason. The foundations and the extent of this natural, as distinct from specifically revealed, knowledge are diversely expressed in different theories. Nevertheless, what distinguishes this approach is that the justification of moral principles without appeal to religious beliefs is acknowledged as possible at least to some significant extent. Indeed, in many of its influential versions the approach regards this knowledge as the basis on which claims to revealed knowledge are to be assessed, at least consistency with what is naturally known being demanded of them.

The recognition of the existence of moral knowledge which, though fully incorporated into religious beliefs, has justification in other terms, demands, of course, reconciling religious claims with a non-religious theory of the foundations of morality. Such non-religious theories are numerous, but traditional religious beliefs put severe constraints on what is acceptable in this context. Most commonly, Christians prepared to accept the idea of natural moral knowledge have subscribed to the view that certain moral principles are, like physical laws, principles on which man, as a matter of fact, is created to live. This means that his life will necessarily conform to these principles, either to his destruction if he flouts the laws, or to his prosperity if he is prepared to acknowledge and live by them. Because moral laws are therefore seen as somehow the fulfilment of man's nature and manifested in human experience, man can by direct examination of that nature and experience discover at least some of these laws. The foundation of morality thus rests on our discovering what is the case about human life irrespective of any religiously revealed expressions of what is or ought to be its concern. The problems, then, are twofold. First, how exactly are we to discover what is the case about human life, and secondly, how precisely does that lead us to conclusions about what ought to be the case in life? It is one thing to argue that morality must have a natural or non-religious basis; it is another to say what that basis is. To this I shall return in due course. But secondly, in asserting the ultimate harmony of morals and religion, Christian belief is here demanding that we set out a basis for a natural morality that fits with its being part of the very nature of things, the nature of man, the universe and God himself. Traditional Christianity, even when it has admitted the existence of natural moral knowledge, has been committed to a doctrine that morality, like science, is concerned to assert ultimate and objective truths. Moral principles, like scientific ones, state what reality is like, for truth is correspondence with reality. How far this restriction can still be accepted must also be examined in due course.

Insisting firmly on the significance of moral and scientific knowledge within a Christian world view is not, I have already argued, the same as insisting that such knowledge must have a religious justification. But giving up that claim can be seen as a first and crucial step to secularisation. Christians have over the centuries had to reconcile themselves progressively to the existence of autonomous sciences and the development of beliefs about the physical world which owe nothing by way of justification to religious beliefs. They have even found a way of accepting this independence of science from religion as central to Christian teaching, an expression of the mandate that God has given to man as called on to 'subdue the earth'. The autonomy of science is therefore seen as built into Christianity rightly understood and indeed as expressly taught in the Bible. In the second approach to moral knowledge that I have outlined, there has likewise been accepted the view that in the moral sphere man has a similar autonomy, it being held that Christian belief rightly understood necessitates this, Biblical teaching about natural morality demanding it too. In both these areas then, in the interests of coherent, defensible beliefs, Christian teaching has had explicitly to recognise the autonomy of the sciences and, at least to some extent, morals. And thus, right there, within its own teaching, Christianity has had to accept two of the most powerful intellectual seeds of secularisation: autonomous scientific knowledge and autonomous moral principles. No wonder the Christian church has found it difficult to cope with secularisation and indeed has itself produced some of the most vocal advocates of, to use Harvey Cox's phrase, 'The Secular City'.[6]

THE CHRISTIAN TRADITION AND THE MORAL LIFE

If we turn from the question of the justification of moral rules and principles to the question of the mechanisms of the moral life, we can, I think, see in this area too how traditional Christian approaches have had to recognise within them certain seeds of secularisation. The mechanism by which men understand what is right and wrong is usually taken by Christians to be in part what is referred to as conscience and in part the activity of reason, though the relationship between these is variously described. Both are thought to be capable of divine illumination and without that both are considered at least liable to be distorted and inaccurate in their appraisals. But knowledge alone is a very passive thing that does not lead to action. The mechanisms that activate men are traditionally seen as internal forces, a cluster of desires and affections that determine all that is done. So central and all determining are these that only by the presence of new desires and affections can the influence of old ones be overcome. What is needed for the moral life is the love of what is true and good and the desire to live by this, not the mere knowledge of what is true and good. But such love and desire must overcome natural loves and desires that all men have and that are opposed to the true and good. To aid the control of these undesirable forces, men are thought to have the internal forces associated with feelings of conscience and a certain power of will. In addition, if all turns on men's desires and affections, then by the deliberate manipulation of the consequences of their actions men can be controlled to some extent externally. If something a man does seeking to satisfy some desire leads to the pain of punishment, a consequence he does not desire, his original desire may be overcome.

The natural functioning of all these mechanisms of reason, conscience, desires, affections and will is, however, thought inadequate for the achievement of the moral life. Just as, in certain extreme forms of traditional Christian belief, natural reason has been thought to be incapable of establishing any valid moral principles, these having necessarily to come from religious revelation, so in the moral life, certain extreme forms of belief have held that no morally good action could be carried out by means of the natural mechanisms that determine human action. Only by specific divine aid, in the development in the individual of new desires and affections directed to fulfilling the will of God and responding in love to him, is the moral life thought possible. Yet just as the extreme claim in justification itself turns out to be untenable, so does this account of the moral life.

To begin with we seem to be faced with the simple fact that, judging by even the most stringent criteria, many men do do morally good actions without any religious considerations being involved. On the basis of natural beliefs, and motivated by desires and affections whose objects are in no sense religious, they act justly and honestly and sacrifice themselves in the interests of others. To argue that these are not really morally good actions is unwarranted and insulting. It is also to win the argument for the necessity of divine aid by definition, so evading the difficulties which the facts present. If, on the other hand, it is argued that these are morally good actions, but that, in spite of their own repudiation of all religious concern, such men are nevertheless acting with specific divine help unbeknown to them, then of course morally good actions can always be said to necessitate this help. We again have one of these solutions to a problem by definition. But this is hardly illuminating. In the first place, if divine help is available, no matter what the religious concern of the agent may or may not be, the significance of religious concerns for the moral life becomes irrelevant and this is not at all what this argument is supposed to show. Indeed, it is because religious beliefs are held to be so crucial to the moral life that this close tie-up between morality and divine help is being maintained. But what is more, if divine help is said to be the cause of every morally good action, though the only evidence of this is the action itself, then the claim surely becomes empty; we are being told nothing. Take a parallel case, in which it is claimed that the reason why people fall asleep is always due to some influence X, though the only evidence for X is that people fall asleep. What this asserts is simply that men fall asleep because of some influence that makes them fall asleep. As an account of why men fall asleep the claim is vacuous. Only if we have some way of recognising X that is independent of people's falling asleep can we discover whether or not X does occur in any or all cases where people fall asleep. Likewise in the question of divine help in the moral life. The claim is empty and tells us nothing unless there is some way, other than the moral life itself, by which we can recognise the existence of divine help. I am not arguing that there is no such thing as divine help in the moral life, rather that we can only claim this with some meaning and justification if we can identify 'moral achievement' and 'divine help' by distinct criteria, and not by defining the first in terms of the second. This means too that the possibility of moral achievement without divine help must be recognised and the mechanisms of moral achievement must therefore be describable in natural non-religious terms. Of course, as a matter of fact it could turn out that in every case of moral achievement we can also discern the presence of divine help, but this is a matter for careful consideration when we have distinct criteria, not for definitional assertion.

It therefore seems to me that just as natural moral knowledge must be seen as compatible with a Christian account of moral claims, so natural moral actions must be seen as compatible with a Christian account of the moral life. In the case of moral knowledge, I argued that Christians are often misled into quite untenable positions because they confuse the epistemological question of the justification of moral rules and principles with the metaphysical question of their ultimate origin or source. In the case of the moral life, Christians also seem to me to be frequently misled by confusing two distinct questions. On the one hand, there is the question of the mechanisms of the moral life as we are aware of these and can understand them in natural psychological and sociological categories. On the other hand, there is the question of what underlies these mechanisms in a more ultimate and metaphysical sense. This latter question is of particular importance where religious claims are concerned. But it must not be assumed that an understanding of the moral life at the first of these levels presupposes an understanding of the second. If these two levels of understanding are not confused, then it would indeed seem possible to reconcile a natural account, not only of the possibility but of the actuality of moral goodness, with a religious account of ultimate causation that underlies and is expressed in natural mechanisms. Within the Christian tradition, moderates have attempted just this, sometimes using the terms primary and secondary causation to mark the distinction. What a satisfactory account might involve I shall discuss later.

But it must again be noted that such a natural account of the mechanisms must be compatible with Christian beliefs of a metaphysical kind about the nature of man. As was previously suggested, Christians have traditionally subscribed to the existence of an objective, absolute reality, the natural world and man having a defined place within that. Natural truths have been seen as expressing, however inadequately, what is the case independently of human concern about it and, in keeping with this, natural mechanisms have been seen as essentially objectively given in the nature of the world, man and society. Traditional descriptions of the nature of man in such terms as soul, conscience, heart, will, have been taken as asserting the ultimate and distinctive elements within which any natural account of the moral life must be accommodated. As a result, stringent restrictions have been placed on the account of the mechanisms of the moral life that Christians have traditionally been able to accept. How far these can still be accepted will be considered later.

At this stage of the discussion one final point about the Christian approach to the conduct of the moral life must be stressed. As suggested earlier, in the search for a coherent view of its mechanisms Christians have had to recognise and accept the implications of the fact that morally good actions can be achieved by processes that require no appeal to religious beliefs or divine help. That men not only can but actually 'do by nature the things contained in the Law' is Biblical teaching. But this idea of a morally good life that is, at least in part, autonomous is hard for many to admit. It seems to deny the supreme importance of Christian claims. What is more, it demands within Christian teaching recognising the legitimacy of a secular approach to the moral life. Yet this autonomy of moral life must surely be accepted. A legitimate place for secular thought and action has to be granted in any remotely adequate account of Christian teaching. If this emphasises yet again that certain roots of secularisation are to be found in Christianity, let that be recognised. Christian teaching can never hope to be coherent if it denies the legitimacy of living in secular terms. What it has to do is to get clear the place of this form of life within a Christian perspective.

References

1 For fuller discussions of the nature of morality, see:
ATKINSON, R. F. (1969). *Conduct: An Introduction to Moral Philosophy*. London: Macmillan.
BAIER, K. (1965). *The Moral Point of View*. New York: Random House.
BENN, S. and PETERS, R. S. (1959). *Social Principles and the Democratic State*. London: Allen and Unwin. Part 1.
WILSON, J., WILLIAMS, N., SUGARMAN, B. (1967). *Introduction to Moral Education*. Harmondsworth: Penguin Books. Part 1.
2 For discussion of the elements of the moral life, see:
PETERS, R. S. (1973). *Reason and Compassion*. London: Routledge and Kegan Paul.
WILSON, J. (1973). *The Assessment of Morality*. Slough: N.F.E.R.
3 See further HIRST, P. H. (1969). The Foundations of Morality. In Macy, C. (ed.), *Let's Teach Them Right*. London: Pemberton Books.
4 See ROSS, W. D. (1930). *The Right and the Good*. Oxford: Clarendon Press.
5 For a much fuller discussion of the autonomy of moral judgments, see:
RAMSEY, I. T. (ed.) (1966). *Christian Ethics and Contemporary Society*. London: S.C.M. Press.
BARTLEY, W. W. (1971). *Morality and Religion*. London: Macmillan.
6 The most illuminating if somewhat exaggerated discussion of the secularisation element in Biblical teaching is in:
COX, H. (1965). *The Secular City*. London: Macmillan.
There are helpful critical articles in:
CALLAHAN, D. (ed.) (1966). *The Secular City Debate*. London: Macmillan.

CHAPTER 3

The Secular Approach to the Justification of Morality

THE APPEAL TO NATURE

It is one thing boldly to assert the necessity for the justification of moral principles independently of religious claims; it is quite another matter to provide in fact a coherent and adequate justification for a body of such principles. Indeed, the history of ethics is strewn with unsuccessful theories that have tried to do just this. Yet the number of fundamentally different ways of setting about this task is limited and the major pitfalls that must be avoided if any account is to be even remotely adequate to the task have been widely discussed. Several major approaches to the justification of moral principles will therefore be looked at briefly so as to indicate both negatively and positively some of the general lines along which an answer may be sought.[1]

Granted the success and prestige of the sciences as autonomous pursuits, notice must first be taken of attempts to justify a body of moral principles by appealing to scientific truths and scientific method. Once religious considerations are put on one side, it is tempting to argue that, as man is a part of the natural world, moral principles, like physical principles, must be simply a set of empirical generalisations about man and his relationship to his physical and social environment. What man is of his nature and the nature of the world in which he lives must provide the key to the right and wrong way to live, to good and evil, to what ought and ought not to be done. What we must discover are the natural laws of human life, just as we seek the natural laws of the rest of the universe. Of course, psychology, sociology and other human sciences, as well as the physical sciences, will be needed if we are to understand the nature of man and his context. But eventually from these sources we shall have the answer to how we ought to live in a series of scientifically justified natural laws.

But there are fatal flaws in such an approach. To begin with, the idea that man has a given determinate nature that science can make known is an elusive notion. Men as we know them are radically determined in their 'nature' by the societies in which they live. From the earliest years they are socialised into forms of thought, patterns of emotional response, attitudes, values and skills which can take many forms. Which, amongst these many possible alternative ways of life that can be produced, amounts to following man's nature? In one sense all of them must be that, but in another sense none of them is simply that. The laws of man's nature are so inextricably tied into rules of his own making that the two cannot be separated. What is 'given' in man is so open-ended that the specific character of his life, what makes each man the kind of man he is, is largely derived from social factors which are highly variable and subject to a large measure of human decision and control. It is not so much that morality can be derived from human nature, it is rather that we need morality so that we know what sort of people we ought to produce. It is just because there can be no natural law for man, as there can be for the non-socially determined parts of the universe, for minerals, plants, and to a large extent animals, that the issue of morality is what it is.

But there is another and in the end more far-reaching weakness to any approach of this kind. Even if man had a specific determinable nature of, say, appetites and desires that could be satisfied only by living according to certain particular rules or principles, why would it follow that living in this way 'according to nature' is what is morally right? Might it not be the case that man is of his nature nasty and brutish? On what basis could it be asserted that nature ought to be followed rather than inhibited? The point here is that it is one thing to determine what is the case about man and the consequences of certain ways of living. It is quite another to determine which of these ways of living is right. Judging what is the case and judging what ought to be are very different things. What all forms of naturalism do is simply take some particular state of affairs, or human quality, or social rule, and without any justification assert that the pursuit of it is what is good or right. The forms of this are legion. In evolutionary terms, the further evolution of the species, or of harmony with the environment, can be taken as defining what ought to be. In more contemporary terms, social harmony, or mental health, may be set up. To intellectuals the development of reason or language may be seen as distinctive of men and therefore to be developed. Men may be seen as motivated by the pursuit of pleasure and avoidance of pain and morality defined in these terms. But in every case there is a transition from a description of some sort to a moral value judgment that can be called in question. It is precisely this jump from 'is' to 'ought', by confusion, definition, or sometimes inference, that marks all forms of naturalism and it is the lack of justification for this jump that is their downfall. It is common to call this error, following G. E. Moore's discussion of it, the 'naturalistic fallacy', though precisely what he thought was covered by this term is disputed.[2] In a limited form, the fallacy is that of not adequately distinguishing judgments about what the natural characteristics of situations are from judgments that are of another kind, in Moore's view judgments concerned with non-natural characteristics. More widely, it is the failure to distinguish the description of actual and possible states of affairs from their evaluation. Expressed in this way, what is wrong with naturalism is not merely that it mistakenly sees moral questions as scientific questions when they are essentially no such thing. Rather it is that it sees moral questions as being in the end answerable by an accurate description of how things are when description alone is quite inadequate for the business of evaluation. It is therefore no way out of the troubles of naturalism to say that what we need is a fuller picture of the nature of man which will be religious or spiritual as well as scientific. Extend the description of the nature of man as much as we like, that will not provide us with the principles of evaluation we want. Nor is there a way out by describing the nature of God or even of his will. Somewhere, somehow, judgments of values have to be made about what men ought to do, and all the descriptions possible of everything of themselves leave us without a single legitimate value judgment. Unfortunately, our own particular value principles are so ingrained in us that we take many of them to be natural, to be expressing what is obviously right or good and thus to need no defence. We think certain acts of heroism, care, or honesty only need to be described for all of us to recognise their obvious moral value as naturally right. But this is an empty claim; what we need is a justification for jumping from a description of the qualities of these acts to the judgment that they are to be valued. Of course, none of this is to deny the importance of knowing all we can about man and his environment for making valid moral judgments. Knowledge of the facts is necessary; the point is that it is not sufficient. Nor is it being denied that many of the moral principles that naturalists may hold to are excellent principles. What is being said is that naturalism provides no adequate grounds for holding them. In addition, it may be noted that many forms of naturalism attempt to define what is 'good' or 'right' in terms of some simple attribute, as, for example, 'the development of reason', when not only are there many other 'good' things in life that get lost in such ethical theories, but a major error is committed by thinking that any or all of these can define for us what is meant by 'good' or 'right'. An adequate ethical theory must get clear the basis on which we can make valid moral judgments, not unjustifiably assert one basic judgment, however general, and make that the definition of value.

The criticisms there have been of traditional forms of naturalism seem to me to be conclusive. Yet it is now becoming clear that two central truths about morality are implicit in such theories, even if they are misconstrued, and that certain violent reactions to naturalism have gone wrong in overlooking these. First, there is the fact that morality does indeed arise because of the nature of man, even if that nature does not simply define or entail what is morally right. If men are significantly what they are because of the influences of society, that cannot be taken to imply that they are not also significantly what they are by natural endowments. They have certain specific physical characteristics and therefore have particular needs if they are ever to survive. They have certain types of sensations and feelings and are able to develop many forms of consciousness. They come to have wants, desires and interests of many kinds; they can choose ends and plan means to achieving these. It is because men are such beings in the particular environment in which they live that morality arises. If they did not have wants and interests, if these were of a different character, if men were related to the environment in a different way, if they had different forms of sensation, morality might either not exist or have a very different content. It is therefore mistaken to conceive of morality as existing independently of 'what is the case' about man and his environment and what as a matter of fact can be. There are limits to morality, then, set by nature, for what cannot be achieved or done cannot be what ought to be. In the well-worn adage, 'ought' implies 'can'. But also there might turn out to be a limited number of basic wants or interests that are as a matter of fact so universal that certain moral principles relate directly to these rather than to the more variable and open-ended possibilities for human life that turn on particular forms of social development. Certain principles may be basic in that without them other possibilities in human life could not arise. In certain senses, then, morality might well be described as natural. But none of this is to say that the crucial distinction between 'ought' and 'is', 'value' and 'description', can be ignored. What we need is a careful account of the relationship, and a justification of some sort for the claim that certain value judgments cannot but be made by rational beings of our kind in this context.

The second point about naturalism that has recently come to be recognised is that, though evaluation and description are not to be confused, their separation in our thought and discourse is sometimes immensely difficult, and indeed according to some may not always be possible. It is certainly true that we use many terms that are both descriptive and evaluative. 'Courage', 'lie', 'murder' are obvious examples of words used to describe actions and at the same time to pass judgment on those actions. In many such cases we can quite readily separate out the descriptive and evaluative elements. But is this always so? Words for many activities or roles may be socially anchored in such a complex fashion that the evaluative and descriptive elements cannot be disentangled. The concept of 'father' in our own present society is commonly taken as an example. The meaning of the term is acquired by learning to use the word in a large variety of subtly different situations in which attitudes and emotions, roles and relationships all play a part, so that the concept is welded into a web of complex relations with other concepts. The idea of analysing the meaning by separating descriptive and evaluative elements may then seem very naïve. It seems to me undoubtedly the case that our discourse is complex in this way and that fact and value are inextricably interwoven in many of our terms. But what does this show? To my mind it does not show that the distinction between description and evaluation cannot be made, nor does it make that distinction any the less significant. The justification of our evaluations is not the less important because evaluations are so difficult to distinguish. And that our descriptive discourse may be in part inextricably infected by value judgments of which we are not at present aware only shows the complexities of our situation. It offers no reason to accept without justification any values of which we can become aware, even if it points to certain elements of circularity that may arise within the process of justification. That in certain parts of our discourse we can detect such circularity does not mean that we are totally trapped, nor that we cannot become more reasonable both within our concepts and discourse and in the modification of our understanding. We must not be lured into too easy a separation of description and evaluation, but we must equally not be lured into a view that our discourse, even our seemingly descriptive discourse, predetermines our values in a way that puts them beyond rational reappraisal.[3]

I conclude that no answer to the justification of moral principles can be found within any form of naturalism, that fact and value are logically different in kind, that we must eschew every appeal to a solution along these lines however attractive it may seem, yet somehow do justice to the rooting of morality in the human and natural context which gives it its *raison d'être*.

THE APPEAL TO INTUITION

But how then are we to proceed, where are we to find a more satisfactory approach? G. E. Moore, who was so critical of naturalism, sought the answer in the notion that just as men are capable of judging by intuition the natural qualities objects and situations possess (for instance, their colours, shapes and sizes), so they are capable of judging by a similar intuition that certain situations possess the non-natural quality of goodness. In this distinctive form of moral intuition lies the basis of our principles, and it is a basis that clearly dissociates moral judgments, not only from natural or scientific judgments, but from religious judgments as well. Morals are indeed autonomous. The point of this parallel between natural and non-natural properties is that in the end moral properties are not definable in properties of any other kind and that judgments about them are as *sui generis* as judgments about, say, colour.[4]

If this parallel could be substantiated, it would indeed provide a basis for morality as objective as that for our knowledge of natural properties, but one not confusing the natural with the non-natural. Unfortunately, the more the parallel is examined the more unacceptable it becomes. The heart of any intuitionist theory is that certain judgments are basic, they are what they are and have no need of further justification. That a particular object is green is said to be intuitively known. But that this judgment of colour is accepted is dependent on many conditions that surround the situation. There is a whole classificatory system for colours that is presupposed. This depends on our ability to agree not only to use certain words in certain situations, but to agree on what these terms distinguish in a complex network of experience. When there is disagreement, there are recognised principles for settling disputes in terms of standard colour charts, the need for normal lighting conditions and so on. When it comes to moral judgments on situations, where is the necessary underlying agreement in judgments? What exactly a term like 'good' picks out is not something we are aware of in terms of a quality or property on which we are able to agree as to when the term applies and when it does not. That there is nothing 'given' on which we agree is just the trouble, and to assert that we do agree when we so frequently do not is not helpful. That this is so is confirmed by the lack of standard agreed procedures as to what to do when disagreements do arise. It may be replied that to ask for all this in morals is to demand too much, for not all men agree about colours and some are indeed colour-blind. Disagreement in that context is not taken as showing that there is no area of objective judgment. Unfortunately, the parallel collapses here too, for we have very good grounds where colours are concerned for saying which group amongst those who disagree has knowledge in this area and which group has not. Colours are so connected with other properties in the world that the information colour-seeing people say they perceive can be checked by corroborating evidence. There are also very good explanations possible as to why the colour-blind are colour-blind. Where moral disagreement is concerned, no such corroborative evidence as to who is possessed of knowledge and who is not is available. This form of intuitionism is a bold and daring claim. Unfortunately, there seems every reason to think it an elaboration of empty assertions that offer an attractive but spurious base to morality by inventing not only special qualities for the job, but also intuitive judgments about them, when there is really no ground for accepting that any such apparatus functions within our moral thought and experience. It is also true that, in asserting the existence of these properties, Moore was in fact merely replacing certain forms of naturalism by another version of it. If moral judgments are a matter of judging the occurrence of certain properties, the evaluation is again a form of description. Not a description of the natural, to be sure, but a description nevertheless. The ultimate weakness of naturalistic theories is that they fail to keep the distinction between description and evaluation, and thus in the end fail to provide any real justification for the evaluations they are seeking to establish. In practice, of course, intuitionism of this kind provides no way of achieving any objective moral judgments, it merely encourages people to dig in their heels and assert the ultimate validity of their own beliefs and the moral blindness of those who disagree.

But even this unsatisfactory theory emphasises an important feature that any acceptable theory of autonomous objective moral judgments will necessarily have. As in other areas of objective judgment, there will have to be certain basic moral judgments about which there is agreement, which have a status parallel to that of judgments of colour where that natural property is concerned. The trouble with the account that has been criticised is that it attempts to force a parallel by inventing another type of property. In morals the judgments are surely not about properties but are made in quite another way because they are evaluative and not descriptive. Nevertheless we need to see whether or not there are certain basic objective moral evaluations on which any understanding of morality rests, just as our understanding of the world rests in part on basic objective colour judgments.

In certain other forms of intuitionism, associated with the names of H. A. Prichard and W. D. Ross, a parallel between moral principles and mathematical and logical principles was suggested.[5] Again, there are difficulties if the similarities are pushed in the wrong way, for just as moral judgments are not quasi judgments about qualities, nor are they quasi mathematical or logical judgments. There is no need to explore the particular difficulties here. For our purpose the prime lessons to be learnt from intuitionism are two. First, that moral judgments must be examined in their own right in an attempt to discover whether or not there can be found in them any of the features that are necessary for objectivity in this area. Secondly, that if there is an autonomous area of objective morality, agreement on certain basic principles of morality will have to be shown to be not only possible but necessary.

THE DENIAL OF OBJECTIVITY

In a previous section it was argued not only that the development of secularisation necessarily involves the search for a non-religiously based account of morality, but that any adequate Christian view of morality also necessitates the provision of such an autonomous base. In commenting on naturalism and intuitionism, I have been concerned to assess how adequate their approach was. If either of these had delivered what it set out to produce, it would have provided an objective form of justification which both total secularists and Christians recognising the place of secular thought in morality could have shared. It is, however, a mark of much contemporary secular thought about morality that it rejects the idea that any adequate objective basis for moral judgments can be found. Such a secular view of morality is not readily compatible with an acceptance of a legitimate place for secular morality within the Christian tradition. Even if a recognition of the autonomy of morality is a necessary part of a defensible Christian approach, the traditional Christian view of that autonomous morality is that its principles must be capable of being viewed as an expression of the will of a wise and intelligent creator. If moral judgments are ultimately matters, not of objective value but of merely human desire, then such secular morality is compatible with a Christian approach only if Christian teaching is very radically re-interpreted in a way that most Christians would find totally unacceptable. Certain central doctrines of Christianity are usually considered to turn in part on the existence of an objective moral demand which men do not meet, even if there is disagreement as to how best that demand is expressed. To see this objective demand simply as a call to a non-objective decision or commitment is, to say the least, hardly a Biblical way of expressing it. Whatever else Christian teaching has traditionally stood for, it has been for both a very particular form of morality and its objective status. But a radical re-interpretation of Christian morality is necessary only if there is a non-objective approach to morality which carries conviction, or if objectivity is shown to be unattainable. The latter seems to me to be very far from the case, in spite of the failures of naturalism and intuitionism to provide a positive account. Nevertheless, their failure and that of other objectivist theories is at least good reason to examine certain central aspects of non-objective theories so as to assess, if only in very general terms, the force of this approach.

The heart of most non-objective theories is the belief that in some form or other moral judgments of right and wrong, or good and bad, state or express only personal or group attitudes or opinions. These attitudes or opinions are simply what they are; they themselves cannot be assessed as right or wrong in any objective sense for it is our attitudes that constitute assessments of value. What we believe to be the facts of any situations can, at least in principle, be shown to be true or false. Not so our attitudes which we express or state in moral terms, for these, though they can be changed, cannot be judged true or false. Our attitudes are personal responses to situations, not recognitions of any further truths about those situations.

In his emotive theory of ethics, C. L. Stevenson developed what is now regarded as the classic statement of this approach.[6] Put cryptically, the central point is an account of the meaning of 'X is good' in terms of two contributory elements: 'I approve of X—do so as well.' What is apparently a statement of a moral judgment is said to be in fact an expression of the speaker's attitude of approval of X and an attempt to influence the attitude of others to it. What moral judgments express are emotional responses not truths, and moral terms have acquired a tendency to produce affective responses in others. When people disagree in their moral judgments on a situation, they might, of course, be simply disagreeing about the facts of the case and not really disagreeing in their moral attitudes. Sort out the facts and they might well agree. But then again they might not, in which case there is genuine moral disagreement. There might still be argument in which one person tries to show that the other is inconsistent in his own attitudes. But assuming the disagreement is not resolved in that way, it is not then capable of resolution by rational debate, for there just is an irreducible difference in their responses. Of course, each can attempt to change the attitude of the other to the situation by any means available, but there is no question of one attitude being objectively right and the other wrong, or of one person being mistaken in his attitude. The two disagree in that they just do respond differently. Moral agreement on this view arises from the fact that men do in general respond emotionally in much the same way to many situations. Where they do not, and misunderstandings and confusions are not responsible, seeking to influence the attitudes of others is all that is possible.

There are two great attractions in this thesis. It seems to face squarely the genuine problems of moral disagreement and to account for our seeming intellectual impotence in such cases. It also takes seriously the emotional aspects of morality, recognising the intense involvement of people in their moral positions and the need to see moral discourse as concerned with changing people's feelings and actions and not just their intellectual outlook. If people's emotional responses are changed, then presumably they will be motivated to act differently. But can the theory's radical rejection of the cognitive nature of moral judgments be critically sustained? I think not. There seems little wrong with asserting that in moral disagreement people disagree in their attitudes. But it is not obvious that by that we mean that they necessarily differ in their emotional responses. They may or they may not. Indeed, one of the significant things about moral judgments is that one's emotional response may be pro what one judges to be morally wrong. If moral judgments are a matter of emotional response, it is therefore going to be necessary to pick out which particular emotions it is that are expressed in moral judgments, and it must also be held that judgments can persist when the emotions have ceased to operate. The claim that there are certain particular 'moral emotions' I will return to shortly. What can be asked immediately, however, is whether or not it is true that the central significance of moral terms is the expressing and evoking of emotions and not the making of cognitive judgments. I see no reason to accept this. Words like 'good', 'bad' and 'ought' might well have emotive meaning as used in many contexts, but that is not to say that they always necessarily have that meaning, or that they are not also centrally terms expressing a cognitive judgment which may be objective. Many statements of simple empirical fact can at the same time be forceful expressions of emotion. When they are, there is no need to deny the factual content; indeed, a recognition of the factual content is usually central to the emotional significance of the statement. Why should this not be the case in moral discourse? The discourse is certainly on the surface concerned with making statements as much as with emotional expression. Much moral debate is engaged in with the deliberate intent of removing the discussion from concern for emotional responses to a concern for making judgments on rational grounds. Indeed, is not this desire more characteristic of moral discourse than that which emotivists suggest? The desire to influence others may be much less the point than trying to make a defensible judgment for oneself—one just wants to know what is right. That strictly moral terms are necessarily and only emotive is assumed by the theory and not shown, and the evidence against such a view is considerable.

When we speak of a person's moral attitudes we may indeed in part be referring to his emotional commitment, but we are certainly also referring to his beliefs, and we regard his attitudes as needing justification, as something for which he ought to have good reasons. Again, when we seek to change people's moral attitudes, we do not usually think of ourselves as directly trying to change their emotional responses so much as trying to change their beliefs, and trust that their emotions will ultimately follow suit. On the emotivist theory, moral argument is in the end a matter of psychological, causal manipulation, shifting emotional responses, not a matter of shifting understanding by producing valid reasons for another judgment. Indeed, in the end valid reasoning in moral matters is not relevant; all there is is persuasion that is or is not effective in changing responses. There are no relevant objective criteria as to whether what is effective also constitutes a valid argument. Whatever else we say of such an account, it certainly runs counter to everything most of us see ourselves as centrally engaged in in the moral pursuit.

But emotivism gets into this position because it does not focus on the fact that every emotional response of a moral kind presupposes a cognitive moral judgment. Rather than emotional responses being the heart of, the source of, our moral judgments, our emotional responses in this as in all other contexts are rooted in our intellectual beliefs about situations. It is not that we simply are disgusted or revolted by the sight of the infliction of pain and that this is expressed in the judgment that the activity is wrong. Indeed, in some circumstances the infliction of pain does not so revolt us. Rather we judge the infliction of pain to be wrong in certain circumstances and are therefore disgusted or revolted. When we learn new facts about a situation, our emotional response can change from being one of disgust to being one of pity or concern. Emotivism takes too simple a view of emotions. We do not just have certain direct emotional responses to situations that are expressed in moral discourse. We have a vast variety of emotional responses that are tied to our personal beliefs and intellectual understanding of situations. What makes our emotional responses what they are is determined by what we judge is the case. We are not morally disgusted and so judge the action as wrong: it is because we judge the action wrong that we are morally disgusted. A correct understanding of the relationship between cognitive judgments and emotions reveals that there can be no adequate emotive theory of ethics, as any adequate grasp of the distinctiveness of the emotions that are seen as the basis of morality raises the unavoidable question of the basis of the cognitive judgments those very emotions presuppose. I see no escape from the fact that, however emotive moral discourse may often be, it is essentially cognitive at its core, and also that moral argument at its core is concerned with changing beliefs and not directly concerned with changing emotions.

Emotivism is important amongst ethical theories for boldly asserting that the kind of meaning moral terms have is in the end non-cognitive. What appear to be moral statements are held not to be in fact statements; they thus make no claims to be true or false and cannot be judged objectively. They are in fact seen as utterances of another kind. It has been argued above that this move in denying the cognitive character of these statements and in asserting the necessity of their emotive character is simply one large mistake. In recent ethical theory a more modest approach of this kind has had its supporters who have simply argued that, whatever one says about the cognitive character of moral judgments, they do in fact have some other function, and if this is not the expression of emotion, then it must be something similar. In particular R. M. Hare has argued that all moral discourse is prescriptive, indicating a commitment on one's own part to act in certain ways and a form of command to others to act similarly.[7] A new sensitivity to different types of 'language game' makes it attractive to tie the idea of moral evaluation to some use of language other than that of simply making statements. Maybe all moral discourse can be seen as commanding others, or, even if it does not do that, maybe it commends or exhorts. What seems to me mistaken is to see any of these particular non-statement uses of language as necessary to moral discourse. To begin with, any of these uses can, I think, be shown to be missing in certain cases where moral judgments are being expressed, just as the emotive element can be shown to be missing in some thoroughly moral contexts. But further, just as moral emotions presuppose cognitive moral judgments, so these other forms of moral meaning are, I think, only intelligible because they presuppose meaningful moral statements. If this is so, then the heart of morality rests in certain cognitive moral judgments and no coherent approach to morality can evade the fundamental question as to the foundation of these judgments. This is not to say that all moral discourse is only a matter of making statements. That is clearly false, for we are all familiar with moral commands, questions, promises, expressions of emotion and so on. What it is to say is that none of these other forms of meaning is necessary to morality, that moral evaluation is not reducible to any or all of them, and that in fact they all presuppose what is necessary: a form of cognitive judgment that can only be logically expressed in a moral statement.[8] The link between moral judgment and action is too tight if concepts like 'ought' and 'wrong' are considered necessarily emotive or prescriptive. They are of themselves necessarily only cognitive in content. But that is not to say they are without any binding significance for us. In cognitive matters concerned with empirical fact, to have reasons for something's being true is to have reasons for believing it even if we do not believe it. So, in moral matters, to have reasons for something's being right is to have reasons for doing it even if we do not in fact do it.[9] The binding force of moral terms is not peculiarly prescriptive, and the appeal to something non-cognitive as characteristic of moral discourse seems to me mistaken.

Emotivism and all other ethical theories that deny the essentially cognitive nature of moral judgments are particular forms of subjectivism, in that they allow no place for reason and objectivity. To reject all such theories as inadequate and in the end incoherent is thus to reject these forms of subjectivism. But even if it is accepted that moral judgments must be cognitive in character, it can still be maintained that nevertheless they are in the end all subjective because we simply do not have any objective grounds on which to base one cognitive judgment rather than another. On this view, morality is based on principles which we have to admit lack objective justification and which are therefore in fact simply matters of opinion, belief, or decision. An individual's morality, or that of a society, is then characterised by the particular principles that determine what ought to be done, but no ultimate justification for those principles is considered possible. Of the different patterns of life that are possible, none can therefore ultimately be regarded as better than any other in any objective sense. This idea of a variety of alternative moralities is regarded by some as the very negation of the idea of morality. Others, however, have claimed that it is of the essence of morality to recognise that ultimately no reasons can be given for decisions on what to do, that we are faced fundamentally with free choice and we are in a situation in which we make ourselves and our social world by our free commitment.

But is this account of the human predicament correct? Is it true that there are no objective grounds on which we can base a set of principles for actions? Does morality necessarily split into a host of distinguishable subjective moralities for individuals or groups, so that right or wrong, good or bad, can only be judged relative to a particular context? Although such a view is nowadays widely subscribed to at least in theory, and many seem to regard it as obviously true, I suggest it is in fact far from being obviously true, that it is difficult even to make coherent sense of the position, and that there are indeed good reasons to think that the search for objectivity in morals is not vain.

The subjective nature of morality is frequently taken to be obvious because of the great diversity of the patterns of human society that anthropologists and sociologists have discovered. Activities one society regards as morally desirable, another regards as morally objectionable, and there is no obvious basis on which to settle the issue. To this day even within our own society different social groups hold opposing views on many matters, issues of sex relations, abortion, gambling, management/labour relations being obvious examples. But mere diversity, even wide diversity, of opinion does not of itself mean that there can be no objective grounds on which to settle these matters. It may be that some individuals or communities live on subjective principles when objective grounds for deciding what to do are nevertheless available. In matters of belief about the physical world, the truth does not even now always find wide acceptance. Again, it may be that, though in principle objective grounds for settling certain moral problems do exist, as a matter of fact the issue is so complex in its ramifications that we have not as yet been able to sort the matter out. In questions about the physical world, many things which we have every reason to think we can come to understand we do not as yet understand. If there is indeed wide disagreement on some moral issues, maybe this should not hide from us wide areas of agreement on other issues on which some measure of objectivity may have been reached. Apparent diversity might also in some cases arise, not from differences in moral principle, but from the important differences in the situations in which the same moral principles are being applied. Change the context radically from a small tribe to that of a large industrial society and quite different decisions about property, finance, sex relations and many other matters might arise from the same moral principles concerning, say, equality of treatment, freedom, protection from suffering. For these, and no doubt many other reasons, the fact of the diversity of moral principles cannot be taken to imply their necessary subjectivity. That many existing moralities are at present in large measure subjective is not to the point, either. At most, diversity can be taken to imply a certain relativity in particular moral judgments, but that of itself would be compatible, not only with the possibility of an objective basis for morality, but even with a universally accepted objective code. As has already been indicated, circumstances alter cases.

But it is doubtful if coherent and consistent subjectivism can be maintained.[10] One common incoherence arises in the attitude many adherents of this position take to those with whom they disagree. If X is right as judged by man A, but wrong as judged by man B, and there is no objective ground on which to decide between these judgments, many conclude that tolerance for A and B to act differently is what ought to follow. But why should this be? A can at best make a subjective judgment about tolerating what B does; what B will decide about tolerating A's actions cannot be prejudged. There can

be no objective ground for thinking he should also side with tolera-
tion. If all principles are subjective, so is that of tolerance. For A to
hold that he has no more justification for his view than B, and that
therefore he must tolerate what B does, is fine for him, but why should
B accept a similar principle? If A begins to hold that B should also
be tolerant for the same reason, is A not admitting some objective
basis outside subjective decisions for determining what should and
should not be done? In consistent subjectivism, no independent
ground of this kind can be admitted.

This is, however, only one example of the difficulties any out and
out subjectivism must face. The problem is at heart that in morality
we are implicitly looking for reasons for what we do, reasons that are
general in character and ultimate. A set of principles may simply be
accepted as providing reasons at one level, but if these are once seen
as themselves lacking justification they quickly cease to have for us
the status appropriate to morality. Further, to settle for a subjectivist
position is to settle for a limit to reason and objectivity. Yet consistently maintaining that limit, by rejecting all attempts to defend
one's principles further, seems arbitrary when the principles we are
concerned with are of their nature being given the importance of
ultimate principles. Thus, if morality is implicitly a matter of having
reasons for what we do, subjectivism involves the assertion that
beyond a certain level of argument reasons cannot be found, and it
thus calls in question the whole moral enterprise.

What these comments on the unsatisfactoriness of emotivism and
other forms of subjectivism throw up is the centrality of the question
as to whether or not the search in morality for an objective basis in
reason for what we do is or is not vain. Neither naturalism nor
intuitionism has elucidated an adequate basis, but a flight into subjectivism is an unsatisfactory attempt to evade the question, not an
answer to it. We must therefore return to the problem as to whether
or not within all the complexities of our moral discourse we can
discern such a basis, however inadequately we may devote ourselves
to having properly grounded principles or living by them when we
have found them.

A RATIONAL ACCOUNT

In trying to present the nature of moral reasoning and its objective
basis, naturalism fails because it makes the unjustifiable demand that
moral reasoning be a form of scientific reasoning. Moore's form of

intuitionism fails because, though it rejects the reductionism of naturalism, it insists that moral reasoning must nevertheless tightly parallel scientific reasoning even to the extent of being about properties. Later intuitionists took the model of another form of accepted objectively valid reasoning, that in mathematics. Such paralleling is helpful in so far as it can lead to an account of moral reasoning that preserves objectivity, but it can be misleading in so far as features that are relevant only to reasoning about the physical world, or about mathematical entities, are also inadvertently and illegitimately incorporated into that account. It is therefore crucial that, in examining moral discourse to see if there are in it characteristics which might secure its objectivity, the parallel with features in reasoning about the physical world, or in any other form of reasoning, be pushed no further than the demand for objectivity necessitates. The relevant features in each case may well be very different, but their logical significance in each discourse must be the same—the securing of objectivity.

If we examine discourse about the physical world, it can be seen that its objectivity is rooted in adherence to certain fundamental principles that are built into the very meaning of the terms we employ about the world. That an object is round or red is, because of the very meaning of the term, a matter of observation by the senses. The rules for the use of these terms must be adhered to and matters of dispute about their application must be assessed in the only way legitimate, by observation. To break the rules for the meaning of the terms, to refuse to settle a matter of dispute by observation, is to opt out of the principles necessary for objectivity. Of course, this is only an example of a principle necessary to the use of reason in this area, but it is an example of a principle which, if it is repudiated, makes reason and objectivity impossible. Kant, and many other philosophers since him, have been concerned to articulate in great detail the principles of this kind that underlie our knowledge of the physical world, principles about which we have no choice, but which are there within all our thought and experience of the world, indeed in terms of which such thought and experience are constituted.

When it came to morality, Kant considered one supreme principle to have a not dissimilar role, a principle to which all reasoned moral rules necessarily conform. In its most famous expression, the principle asserts that one can only be rational in one's actions if one acts on a rule 'which you can at the same time will that it should become a universal law'. To act on a rule that one does not accept as universally applicable is, on this view, to opt out of being rational about one's actions. Just what this principle means has been disputed, but it would seem to be making certain points that are indeed true of our reasoning about actions. Surely it is irrational for me to approve of my acting in a way that I do not also approve for anyone else in this or a similar situation. If it is right for me to take this money, it is right for anyone else in the same situation. Also, if it is right for me to act in this way, it must be right even if I am at some other point in this situation. If it is right for me to take this money from one of my friends, it must be right for someone else to do this when I am in the position of the friend. If this principle is not adhered to, then indeed reason would seem to disappear from the determining of my actions. Nevertheless, there are real difficulties in this very abstract and formal demand. Many very trivial rules that would hardly seem matters of morality can be 'universalised' in this way. By playing up the uniqueness of situations, and of my own characteristics in particular, it can be argued that almost any rule that suits me is universalisable. But, even if one could get round these difficulties by more careful formulation, it is undoubtedly true that the principle is at best necessary, but not sufficient, for a fully rational morality. I might be prepared for the universal application of my totally idiosyncratic practices even with me in another role, but that alone hardly makes the position objectively defensible.[11]

The view that reason can get us no further in moral matters has been forcefully defended in contemporary eithcs, but significant attempts have been made to explore the notion of reasons for actions still further. In particular, it has been argued by Professor R. S. Peters that a number of other principles are implicit in this notion and that if one is to have reasons for what one does, one is committed to these.[12] Again, it is held that to deny these is thereby to be irrational. He instances a commitment to a principle of fairness or impartiality by which people are treated the same unless there are relevant differences between them. Differences in treatment can only be justified by reference to differences in the situations. In a similar way it can be seen that, without adherence to a general principle of truth-telling, determining actions by reasons is necessarily vitiated. Again, acting on reasons is only consistently applicable if it is accepted that people shall in general be free to act as they determine. In addition, it must not be forgotten that the content of morality, what it is concerned with, is the actions of people with particular interests. A consideration of those interests, and a recognition that those of others are as significant for them as one's own interests are for oneself, is therefore another demand if it is human actions that are to be rationally determined. In this way, if morality is about having reasons for actions, the very notion of 'reasons for actions' itself lays down a number of fundamental principles without which the whole search for reasons is unintelligible. These principles are therefore not optional, or matters of choice or decision for the person who demands reasons; they are principles to which he is unavoidably committed by making the demand for reasons. What these do is map out certain fundamental features of rational morality, laying bare what objectivity in this area necessitates. In so far therefore as we look for reasons for actions and persist in this pursuit, not being deflected by various forms of arbitrary unjustified dogmatism, we will find ourselves having to agree on at least certain principles beyond which reason cannot go. All rational men must therefore accept principles of fairness, truth-telling, freedom, consideration of interests, and respect for persons. At least these are the foundation planks of rational morality.

There are, of course, a number of important objections which can be made to this account, two of which in particular seem to me to help us focus on just what the theory is saying. First, it can be argued that what is happening here is that Peters is dogmatically saying: these are the principles that underlie what I call morality, so that all reasoning must begin with these, and if anyone lays down any other basis, I do not call that morality. In other words, the position is finally pinned down by a subjective decision for which there is no justification. This is, however, an erroneous account of the thesis. Peters is not himself arbitrarily laying down as a basis one set of principles from which reasoning can take place, thus setting up one form of morality when many other forms could be developed from alternative sets of principles. He argues rather that, if anyone pursues consistently having reasons for actions, that person will be driven back to these principles, and that these can be shown to have an ultimate status. Whatever principles anyone might put forward in morality, we have a right to ask for their justification, and if that is not produced we have no grounds for accepting these principles rather than any others. When the justification for Peters' principles is asked for, he argues by what is technically known as a 'transcendental deduction' that the principles, far from being arbitrary, are necessary to the pursuit of reasons for actions. They are shown to be, not a personal assertion of what is being taken to be ultimate, but an account of what all rational men must accept as ultimate in our concern for reasoned actions. Reasons for all principles can legitimately be asked for, even for the fundamental principles, the justification for these being the demonstration that the notion of reason for action presupposes them.

But this reply can lead to the second criticism. What is being spelt out is simply what is implicit and necessary to reasoning about actions as we have it, and that is only to express our idea of rational morality, something which has no objective status after all. Other societies have developed different forms of reasoning about actions and these have had implicit necessary features which were built into the relevant concepts and discourse just as Peters' principles may be built into our own. Are we not therefore being given an account of a morality that is still subjective in a very real sense, one relative to our society? What is here being argued is undoubtedly true in part. Peters' principles are an attempt to articulate reasoning about actions as we have developed it. In other times and places, and to some extent in our own society, other concepts and patterns of reasoning can be found. What does not follow from this, however, is that the whole procedure is therefore totally subjectively determined and totally relative.

Perhaps this can best be seen by recognising that all our understanding, even our scientific knowledge, suffers from exactly the same problem. Our understanding of the physical world in scientific terms has developed with certain implicit principles that constitute reason in this area. In other times and places the physical world has been reasoned about in other ways: for example, in complex forms of magic and in primitive religions, which have had other implicit principles. Yet none of this shows that science is totally subjective (it is just our way of reasoning and no more objective than any other), or that everybody is right in his own terms. Conceptual schemes that give us understanding are not simply subjective inventions to which our experience has to conform. They are indeed human constructs, but they are necessarily developed in relation to experience to carry out certain functions within that experience. In science, the concepts have the role of making sense of the observable world and that world itself is something given, it is not of our inventing, even if we can understand it only through conceptual apparatus we must ourselves develop. The implicit principles of science are what they are because of the particular relationships of the concepts with that to which they apply. If concepts were not developed to pick out what is observable, in terms of principles whereby the concepts can be judged to apply or not apply in observation, scientific understanding would not exist. What are to be found in the fundamental principles of science are the rules of a form of understanding that we have developed, one that to a greater or lesser degree coherently fits an area of our experience. Conceptual schemes may be modified to obtain a better fit with elements of experience. But only where we have concepts that can be judged to apply or not in experience do we have a form of understanding. Different conceptual schemes that are concerned with the same type of experience will, of course, necessarily involve the same fundamental principles. But all that one can ask of a form of understanding is that there be concepts so related to experience that in any particular case their application can be judged. If another society appears to have a quite different form of understanding, we can therefore only examine its concepts and their application and assess its success within these terms. What I am insisting is that objective understanding or reason is not what any group makes it, it is only present in conceptual schemes with certain necessary features, when there are objective rules governing the application of the concepts in experience. How far some form of understanding in a primitive society offers an objective explanation of observable events can only be assessed by examining the characteristics of the interpretation. We cannot assume it is, say, simply bad science, as the function of the discourse may not be to give that kind of explanation. The way the concepts work, and the basis on which judgments are made, need to be looked at in their own right. But that is not to say that any form of explanation is acceptable. Some forms of explanation are not so developed that they can be objective. Others indeed are objective in form, but what they maintain is simply false within the system's own principles.

Clearly, men have developed many different conceptual schemes and we can only find out their character by looking at the principles which are implicit within them. It may not always be easy to determine whether any given scheme is so related to experience that its judgments are objective; indeed complex schemes may be partially ambiguous or inconsistent in their objectivity. We must not be too hasty in totally denying the existence of some limited objective grasp within the working of certain concepts. The history of human thought should make us cautious, for out of uncertain gropings might emerge genuine understanding. At present we have certain specifiable forms of understanding, but these surely can, and no doubt will, change. Understanding in science with its present form of conceptualisation would seem to be limited and new forms could emerge from, say, the inadequacies of fundamental physics. Our present forms of reasoning may have limits and weaknesses that will one day seem as inadequate as forms of reasoning men have already discarded. We can therefore only unearth the character of reason as we have thus far achieved it, and, if further developments can be expected, recognise that not all new conceptual variations will necessarily prove acceptable. That the nature of reasoning in science is in a state of development, and that any account of it is therefore only a report of the features of what we at present have, does not in any way make science subjective. It remains supremely the example of a pursuit that has developed high objectivity in its judgments. And this is true even if there now seem to be clear limits to the objectivity that this specific type of understanding can have.

The implications of this discussion for the Peters account of morality are, I think, that he has articulated at least some of the fundamental principles of the discourse we have so far developed in which we give reasons for actions. It seems to me that judgments on actions in these terms, attending to the issues of freedom, truth-telling and so on as the principles set out, are at least in some measure judgments of an objective kind. No doubt moral understanding can and will develop a more adequate objectivity, just as science has in the past and no doubt will in future. But the force of the trans-cendental deductions is the claim that reasoning is here being anchored in judgments where concepts are applied in as objective a manner as we have so far developed. Of course, objectivity in reasons for actions is anchored in principles that differ from those anchoring objectivity in judgments about what is the case in the physical world. Deciding how to act is not like looking to see. But the force of Peters' approach is the search for that objectivity in morality in features logically equivalent to those that provide it in other areas. In under-standing the observable world, those are principles that are implicit in what it means to have reasons for judging what is the case. In moral understanding, they are principles that are implicit in what it means to have reasons for judging what to do.

Peters' account of the basis of morality claims to be no more final than any account we might give of the basis of science. Both are developing forms of understanding. What is more, understanding is a pursuit undertaken by beings who themselves are no doubt changing within a context of total flux. There is no reason to suppose that even our notion of understanding itself is fixed; after all, presumably our distant ancestors had no such form of consciousness. Yet none of this alters the character of understanding as we pursue it and the neces-sary place of objectivity within it.

If we must not absolutise any understanding we have and freeze it as if developments in the human mind will not occur, nor must we be seduced into thinking that there is for us no significant difference between objectivity and subjectivity, or between truth and error. What is objectively the case is something we can to a greater or less degree discover within the state of flux and that is not to be simply equated with what we ourselves totally create within that flux. Nor must we imagine that different societies or even individuals are in such different situations within the flux that forms of objectivity and reason must differ. Indeed, there is much to indicate the reverse. Men all the world over are alike in their major physical and mental attributes, their environments differ in only limited respects. Is it surprising then that, if they share conceptualisation, they share many of the forms it takes? The common features of men and their relative stability have even resulted in certain principles of thought that seem to be necessary to all intelligibility. The ultimate status of logical laws as conditions for all that men can coherently think is something that we may well have to recognise, but we must never forget that this is only to say that these laws are ultimate for beings with human characteristics in this kind of context. Within the limits of such laws, various forms of understanding have been achieved. What is objective in any area, including morality, is of its nature universal in significance for all those who can share the conceptual schemes in which it is achieved. It is Peters' claim to have elucidated, at least in part, in what that objectivity in morals consists. If the precise formulation of the fundamental moral principles that Peters has given may be subject to dispute, this approach to the basis of rational morality nevertheless seems to me to be precisely the way in which its foundations can be established. And if the result of this approach must necessarily be a set of principles formulated within a conceptual scheme which is historically and socially relative, it nevertheless sets out the fundamentals of as objective and rational an approach as is available to us.[13]

It has been argued that in certain fundamental principles we have the logically necessary basis of a rational morality. To these the judgments of all men concerned with having reasons for actions must, if they are defensible, conform. In this I am maintaining that the approach outlined by Peters is correct and that, in seeking to pursue reason as far as we are able, we are bound to a body of such principles. The exact formulation of these principles is, however, a difficult matter and they are not at present as clearly expressed as one would like. That we reason with such principles is no guarantee that we can readily disentangle them in a form in which they can be shown to be beyond all doubt necessary to our having reasons for actions. Nor should it be presumed that the principles Peters has given constitute an exhaustive list. Nevertheless, I think we have both an outline of the major principles of rational morality and an outline of a defence of them that faces head on what an adequate defence must involve.

But if the fundamental principles provide the ultimate reasons for what is to be done, they have to be applied in all the many varied situations in which we act. They are therefore expressed in rules about a vast variety of such things as the use of resources, money, industrial and personal relations. It is the whole web of facts about man and his environment to which these principles must be applied. In some cases they relate to matters which are universal human concerns, such as access to food and protection from injury. In other cases they relate to matters peculiar to particular societies or even minority groups (trade union concerns and company directors' expenses would be cases in point). There are thus rules of varying degrees of generality, some of which can be described in Peters' terms as 'basic', others being much more particular. Rules concerned with basic universal interests may well appear obvious and hardly matters of dispute, taking the same form in many if not all societies. Rules dealing with more particular matters may well vary considerably from group to group because of the varying circumstances. Rational morality does not result in the same actions when the attendant facts of situations differ. What is fair distribution of resources in one situation is not necessarily so in another. In that sense, the rules which fundamental principles lead to in one community may justifiably be different from those to which they lead in another. Monogamy may not be defensible in all situations. It was also pointed out earlier that our particular actions are many-faceted, having many implications. In considering what ought to be done, we need to attend to these different aspects, and it is when we come to look at these that the same fundamental principles can lead to very different conclusions according to the contexts.

Nor must it be assumed that there is in the end necessarily only one rationally defensible thing to do in any given situation. Often alternative actions are equally justifiable. The clash of principles when applied in specific contexts may not be resolvable in any one way. Rational morality is based in certain principles, but of the nature of the case these cannot lead to simple universal answers covering all situations. In particular individual cases we may be faced with a simple issue of principle—for example, of fair treatment to individuals in the same position. We may, however, be faced with conflicting rules in which, say, we must try to maximise both truth-telling and consideration for suffering, a problem to which there is no simple answer. Some complex situations are unique and must be looked at in that way. How the principles apply can perhaps only be judged by someone having detailed personal knowledge as a participant in that situation. Often even the participants do not know all the relevant facts. Morality on rational principles is not an easy matter, but then human actions in all their variety and inter-relations are not simple. The idea that there can be any set of rules to apply mechanically is naïve, and the more we understand of situations the less we shall feel that at this stage of human history even a rational morality can begin to give us all the answers. Maybe in principle all the answers can never be known. But that does not take away one jot from the status of the principles we have, by which we can remove large tracts of irrationality from our actions and on which we can positively promote a fair degree of reason.

MORAL PRINCIPLES AND THE SECULAR CHRISTIAN

But what of the Christian view of such a secular morality? I argued earlier that not only must we take seriously the possibility of a defensible non-religiously based morality, just as we now accept non-religiously based science, but that a coherent Christian view of morality positively requires it. This has been implicitly recognised for long by many Christians and is even Biblical teaching. But it has been denied by others, in part because no adequate non-religious base for morality seemed available. Biblical teaching implies that what is right can be naturally recognised, though it gives no indication as to how that recognition comes about. If the Peters' account of morality is defensible, it provides Christians with a justification for objective moral principles. What is more, it is on this view to be expected that by reasoning coherently about actions, even if that reasoning were not very sophisticated, men could readily formulate certain of the fundamental and basic moral rules. That they would seem to be 'natural' describes in a simple term precisely this state of affairs. But just because Christian moral teaching has in fact arisen from this 'natural' base, though this fact has only rarely been recognised, rational morality as Peters outlines it is in all major respects identical with the central tenets of Christian morality. It is part of the genius of Christian teaching that it is in moral matters intensely rational. What this means for the intelligent Christian of our secular age is that he can overtly accept that we have autonomous moral understanding and that, at least as judged on moral terms, Christian teaching is rationally defensible. No longer need the Christian imagine he has to take up the illogical position that he must derive his morality from religious beliefs. Christian beliefs do not justify his morality; his morality is rationally based and this gives him one reason for taking Christian beliefs seriously. At least Christianity is right in its moral elements.

But further, this overt acceptance of secular rational morality means that the contemporary Christian need no longer begin to imagine that there should be something about his moral principles that rational non-Christians must reject. The rational humanist and the rational secular Christian can expect to be in full agreement. This is particularly important in the Christian approach to contemporary moral issues. Questions about, say, contraception, abortion, euthanasia, private medicine, selective education, cannot be settled on any other grounds than those equally justifiable by Christians and humanists. There are no distinctively, yet justifiable, Christian arguments; there are only good reasons. The Christian can best be Christian by refusing to hunt for non-existent rules in Biblical teaching, where in any case there is always the problem of trying to disentangle the fundamental principles within a particular application of them, by rejecting the trend of an often mistaken Christian tradition, and by reasoning the matter out in a thoroughly secular fashion. He can best be Christian by being thoroughly secular. Biblical morality is acceptable just in so far as it is rational morality.

Yet to many Christians who will accept the existence of some moral understanding outside Christian teaching, I must surely seem to be pushing the extent and significance of such knowledge much too far. They would consider that Christian teaching acts as an authoritative norm against which our natural understanding must be judged, and that Christian morality goes beyond any rational understanding by adding further principles. The first of these suggestions I regard as mistaken for, as I argued earlier, an appeal to authority can only be justified if that authority is known to be a moral authority and we have no grounds for judging that outside the use of natural moral understanding itself. The claim that Christian teaching adds further moral principles to rational morality is, I think, in one sense true yet in another false. It is true that the acceptance of Christian beliefs does introduce into practical affairs new considerations that are justifiable only by those beliefs. The use of money for the maintenance of certain religious institutions, the allocation of time to the development of the religious life, or, perhaps more importantly, beliefs about the spiritual nature of man and his relationship to God which might influence judgments about abortion or euthanasia, are examples. Yet here again we have begun to appreciate that, logically, secular rational morality must be the norm by which to judge religious claims and not vice versa. No longer can religious beliefs that run counter to scientific understanding be accepted. Nor can religious beliefs that run counter to rational morality. If therefore a belief about the spiritual nature of man leads to a principle that runs counter to rational morality, what we must logically reject is the religious doctrine and its moral consequences. Where Christian teaching therefore seems to add to rational morality, it does so only in so far as the principles it leads to are compatible with rational secular judgments.

What in effect this does is to make specifically Christian practical principles justifiably operate only within the area where alternative actions are defensible and where no secular moral principles run counter to them. This is in fact to accept the appropriateness of the 'privatisation' of the distinctive features of Christian morality. Public morality must be defensible as applicable to all in the society, and is on these terms a matter of finding rational principles for matters of public significance and not simply a matter of finding anyhow a code of behaviour acceptable to a majority. Principles that rest on religious beliefs, and which are therefore radically controversial extensions of rational morality, are properly matters for individual judgment. What is also entailed in this position is the recognition of the legitimacy of the principle that the practices of religious adherents that have public implications should be subject to the dictates of rational secular morality. Not that public opinion, or the law of the land, at any time necessarily expresses such a defensible morality. Nevertheless, to the secular Christian such critical procedures are proper and to be welcomed, not merely tolerated as examples of an unfortunate decay of religion. The boundary between public and private morality is difficult to draw and turns on the necessity for having interpersonal decisions on certain matters that affect others than those immediately involved. Of course, the private area cannot be equated with that which religious concerns can properly influence. Yet what I am arguing is that only in this area can one rationally accept that religious principles have a decisive influence on action.

It would seem then that on this view Christian teaching must be seen as adding nothing to a rationally defensible morality to which rather it must always be subject. Reason is made supreme, as indeed it always must be even by those who illogically reason otherwise. The doctrine that reason is not in all thought supreme is only defensible if reason is understood in some limited sense to be nothing but, say, scientific reasoning. Without reason and objectivity there cannot be any truth, let alone a higher truth. All there can be is unintelligibility, incoherence and error, and that in morals as much as any other area. In religious belief the same is necessarily so. But can religious beliefs have no legitimate bearing on our moral outlook? Two things at least they do.

First, they do add, within the moral domain, distinctive positive ideals. The distinctive practical principles to which I have referred can and do produce different life styles. They can influence significantly how people spend their time, their money, the relationships into which they enter. The good life in rational terms is not uniquely determined and religious teaching can weight attention to certain particular principles. Thus, even if there is not a defensible distinctive Christian morality, there can be a distinctive Christian life style that is as defensible as the beliefs on which it rests.

But secondly, and much more importantly, Christian beliefs have much to say about the significance of morality. If we can once get away from the idea that the function of religion is to tell us what is right and wrong, accepting that by hard work we can find that out for ourselves, we can focus on the central point of Christian teaching that it is about God, about the religious significance of morality and its place in some ultimate transcendent scheme of things. The importance of religious beliefs is that they make claims to religious truth, not moral truth or scientific truth, though they may presuppose such truths. The Christian claim is that what is morally wrong is not only that, not only something rationally indefensible, it is also sin, a matter of man's relationship with God, a transgression of the ultimate principles of human existence. The Christian thus sees the whole of what is moral as part of an order or purpose wider than the merely moral. Morality is also believed to have its origin or source in God and to be an expression of his will. Yet again, it must be insisted that even if valid, these beliefs do not provide any additional justification for moral principles. It may be a justifiable religious belief that God was in existence prior to the existence of men and their morality, yet their knowledge of morality may be prior to and indeed part of the justification of belief in the existence of God. Religious beliefs may provide additional conceptual support for why people should be moral but they cannot, I think, in fact add any further grounds for that, or for judging whether, say, abortion is or is not right. To take moral principles as justified by the religious beliefs within which they are expressed is precisely to confound the whole logic of our situation, for it is only because we can judge the principles advocated that we have grounds for taking the religious claims seriously. We do what is right because it is justifiable and it is only because it is justifiable that it can figure in religious beliefs we can accept. There is in the end no religious justification for the moral claims of religion.

Yet morality as a whole has a particular status for the Christian. In Christian thought there are concepts and beliefs which draw the believer's attention to an importance for morality that a non-believer will reject. What this does is undoubtedly to underpin the objectivity of morality for the Christian by placing it in a transcendent scheme, making it stand starkly outside himself in its source and significance. To the secular Christian, to live the moral life is a rational thing to do because it is indeed the rational life; for that reason too it is also the life for which he ultimately exists.

I hope it is clear that my account of a secular Christian's view of morality is radically different from that of all those secular theologians who, being total secularists, reduce religious beliefs to nothing more than the moral teaching they encapsulate. Moral judgments are to my mind autonomous and are to be judged valid on their own terms, according to their own unique characteristics. In that case, religious beliefs that incorporate moral teaching cannot be defensibly accepted if they run counter to moral principles that are acceptable on autonomous grounds. But the recognition of those principles and the basis of their justification is all that this position demands of religious beliefs. The truth or error of reductionism, or of more traditional metaphysical forms of Christian belief, is another matter. To make clear that no reductionism is in any way implied, I have assumed a heavily traditional interpretation of Christianity. I see no incompatibility in what I have argued with a thoughtful, considered traditionalism. But if it has not been my purpose to defend religious reductionism, neither has it been my purpose to defend traditional religious beliefs. I have been concerned only to argue for a secular morality and to indicate its compatibility with even a conservative approach to such beliefs. In fact this view of morality demands nothing other than a recognition of the legitimacy of reason and the objectivity it implies. Of itself it makes no demands for any particular metaphysical position other than one in which the pursuit of objectivity is not vain in matters of action any more than in, say, matters of perception. This leaves the door wide open to all those forms of religion, including those interpretations of Christianity, which do not deny the place of reason. Morality approached in terms of reason seems to me the only form that is acceptable in itself. It is also a form which itself leads to a religiously open secular society.

References

1 For a general outline and critique of major contemporary ethical theories, see:
HUDSON, W. D. (1970). *Modern Moral Philosophy*. London: Macmillan.
WARNOCK, G. J. (1967). *Contemporary Moral Philosophy*. London: Macmillan.
WARNOCK, M. (1960). *Ethics since 1900*. London: Oxford University Press.
2 MOORE, G. E. (1903). *Principia Ethica*. London: Cambridge University Press.
3 For a fuller discussion, see:
HUDSON, W. D. (ed.) (1969). *The Is-Ought Question*. London: Macmillan.
4 See MOORE, G. E. (1903). *Principia Ethica*. London: Cambridge University Press.
See also KUPPERMAN, J. J. (1970). *Ethical Knowledge*. London: Allen and Unwin. Chapters 1 and 2.
5 ROSS, W. D. (1930). *The Right and the Good*. Oxford: Clarendon Press.
PRICHARD, H. A. (1949). *Moral Obligation*. Oxford: Clarendon Press.
6 STEVENSON, C. L. (1960). *Ethics and Language*. New Haven, Conn.: Yale University Press.
STEVENSON, C. L. (1963). *Facts and Values*. New Haven, Conn.: Yale University Press.
URMSON, J. O. (1968). *The Emotive Theory of Ethics*. London: Hutchinson.
7 HARE, R. M. (1952). *The Language of Morals*. Oxford: Clarendon Press.
HARE, R. M. (1963). *Freedom and Reason*. Oxford: Clarendon Press.
8 SEARLE, J. R. (1969). *Speech Acts*. London: Cambridge University Press.
9 EDGLEY, R. (1969). *Reason in Theory and Practice*. London: Hutchinson.
10 For a fuller discussion of subjectivism and relativism, see:
WILLIAMS, B. (1972). *Morality*. Harmondsworth: Penguin Books.
11 For an excellent introduction to Kantian ethics, see:
ACTON, H. B. (1970). *Kant's Moral Philosophy*. London: Macmillan.
12 See PETERS, R. S. (1966). *Ethics and Education*. London: Allen and Unwin. Part 2.
13 For a fuller discussion of questions of objectivity in science and other forms of understanding, see:
TOULMIN, S. (1972). *Human Understanding*, Volume 1. Oxford: Clarendon Press.
LAKATOS, I., and MUSGRAVE, A. (eds.) (1970). *Criticism and the Growth of Knowledge*. London: Cambridge University Press.
HAMLYN, D. W. (1972). Objectivity. In Dearden, R. F., Hirst, P. H., Peters, R. S. (eds.). *Education and the Development of Reason*. London: Routledge and Kegan Paul.
HIRST, P. H. (1974). *Knowledge and the Curriculum*. London: Routledge and Kegan Paul.

CHAPTER 4

The Secular Approach to the Moral Life

THE IMPORTANCE OF AUTONOMY

If the moral life is a life informed throughout by certain rules and principles, we must turn now to examine in more detail just what that involves for the individual person. Let us therefore assume that we have an appropriate set of rules and principles, even if they are not exactly those that have been argued for here, as much if not all that will now be outlined is of wider application. Granted that, in what way is it proper to expect that this moral 'order' will function within the individual's life?

First, almost obviously, it is to be expected that his actions will be seen to conform to the rules and principles concerned. But having said that, it must be added immediately that the moral life is of its essence not merely a matter of observable movements fitting in with certain rules. An automaton cannot be a moral being, nor can a trained pigeon, parrot, or rat. For there to be the possibility of moral action, what occurs must be intended by the agent. It must be done by a being who knows what he is doing and, further, it must be done of his own volition. Both these things are necessary. A being might know what is happening, be conscious of situations, recognise objects and movements, yet its behaviour be causally determined in a mechanistic or stimulus-response manner. We would not then consider such behaviour as even up for moral consideration. We can talk of the causes of what is happening in this case, but we cannot meaningfully ask the reasons the being has for doing what it does. But if the being is conscious of what is occurring, and acts of its own volition, so that it itself decides what will occur, then we can ask why this is done rather than that. Only when reasons for actions can properly be asked for, and not merely causes of behaviour, is it possible for a person to be acting morally. When a person both knows what is going on and acts by decision, even if he in fact can give no reason for doing one thing rather than another, the question of morality arises, because the person could have done otherwise and have acted on reason. But if a person not only knows what is going on, decides to act and with reasons, yet it is the case that he cannot determine what occurs, then whatever the physical, psychological and social explanation, the question of morality once more cannot arise. It is where reasons for acting and voluntariness are both possible, even if not appropriately exercised, that actions can be morally judged.[1]

The upshot of these considerations is that, though we can in one sense judge an action by its outward conformity to moral rules and principles, it is only fully seen as a moral action by reference to the person's own intentions, the reasons why he acted in this way. Even if outwardly the action is morally excellent, the person may have done this deed for reasons quite other than that it is justifiable by moral rules and principles. He may have done it without even thinking about what is justifiable, have acted because of his personal desires, or have simply done what someone else told him to do. What he acted on as reasons might thus not provide a moral justification, even if the resulting action is so justifiable. Of course, he may have acted for both defensible reasons and, say, from personal desire as well, but it is only in so far as the action is done for reasons that conform to moral rules and principles that it is an expression of the morally good life.

To characterise moral actions in this way makes the notion of the person's own judgment as to what to do central. The idea of self-direction, self-determination of one's life, is what makes the action one's own, and what makes one morally responsible. To work things out for oneself rather than to act simply out of habit, as conditioned by others, or just on instructions, seems to be necessary to morality, and in so far as one does not do this is one not failing to accept one's very nature as a free being capable of determining what shall be done? As a result of the central importance of this form of freedom in morality, some have argued that this and this alone is what makes an action moral: that it has been decided by the agent totally freely, without any constraints. Morality is, on this view, a matter of total autonomy or freedom of decision. There are, however, overwhelming difficulties with this approach. To begin with, the idea of freedom from constraints is surely a matter of degree and never absolute. Some have sought to imply that we are always, necessarily, totally

and fundamentally free to choose what we will both be and do, even
if we exercise this freedom by drifting with the crowd or living by
habit. But that is to make every piece of behaviour a free act and gets
us nowhere. Yet that even some acts we make are totally free choices
is not defensible either, for it makes no sense to say we choose rather
than plump unless we have acquired some sort of principles or criteria
for deciding. And if that is so, how did we acquire these criteria? Did
we totally freely choose these, too? In practice no, they are the expression of our state of mind whatever the source of that. No choice
we make can in the end be totally free of our characteristics at that
time, and if any act could occur which was independent of all considerations, it could hardly be said to be a choice. What is more, it
would of necessity be totally arbitrary, and why should that be a
moral decision? But if totally free choice is not possible, then the
decisions a person takes are to some extent going to be determined
by his character as a product of nature and upbringing. There may
still be free choice and decision, but these are now based on, and
limited by, ideas and principles already possessed. In that case, the
presupposed principles behind our free choices are crucially important in morality. To pretend these do not exist, or to leave them
unexamined, is to mistake the situation or to be morally irresponsible.

It is tempting, if one rejects the idea that the moral life can be the
totally autonomous life, as there is no such thing, then to argue that
the moral life should be autonomous in the sense that one is subject
to no one outside oneself, one is true to one's own self, does one's own
thing, acts authentically. The snag is still, however, that there is no
reason to suppose that the self that is the basis of these actions is
going to lead to anything we could properly describe as morally good.
It is the case that anarchists and criminals are highly autonomous
and many of them authentically act out their existing characters.
Pure autonomy cannot determine morality, for of itself it is arbitrary
and in practice there is no such thing. When it takes the form of
authenticity, the limits on autonomy do not produce morality unless
the self behind the actions is truly moral. Autonomy, in the sense of
exercising free determinate choice, is necessary to the moral life. But
just because that freedom must always be exercised within constraints that operate within the individual, autonomy is not sufficient for morality. These very constraints are crucially important in
determining the character of the individual's moral life. If these are
geared to the rational determination of behaviour, then all well and
good. If not, autonomy will hardly be likely to produce what is

morally desirable. Authenticity is a necessary part of the moral life only in so far as it overlaps with autonomy, in the sense of the exercise of free determinate choice. When it is involved as providing a total account of morality, it seems to me it implies an uncritical acceptance of each person's existing moral character whatever that might be. The moral life is not to be lived by each person exercising his autonomy in being true to himself. It is lived by exercising one's autonomy in the interests of, and within the limits of, reason. Overstressing the place of autonomy in the moral life comes from forgetting what the precise character of morality as a whole is.[2]

REASON AND THE LIMITATIONS ON AUTONOMY

The principle of freely determining one's actions is fundamental to morality, but it is only one of several prima facie principles necessary to acting rationally. In so far as freedom is allowed its head, and it leads to anything but the rational life, because the legitimacy of other principles is denied, the outcome cannot be morally defensible. If we are to have morality, the principles that provide the limits within which autonomy works must be those of reason. Moral man is free to make his own judgments about actions, but only if he makes them on the basis of the principles of reason will they be morally defensible. In so far as autonomy is necessary to morality, the moral life results only where the autonomy is used to work out what reason demands and to act on that. Freedom to do otherwise exists, of course, but thinking out what to do for oneself and freely acting on it, if reason is ignored or denied, is in no sense conducive to morality. Contemporary cults for deciding for oneself, for being autonomous, or authentic, when not directed by the principles of reason, are necessarily directed by other principles, and there is no reason why they should result in anything but the chaotic permissiveness with which we are all too familiar.

For all that I have said, however, it might still be questioned whether or not autonomy even within the limits of reason is necessary to the moral life. Might not the moral life best be lived by conforming to many social and institutional roles? The latter exist independently of any one individual and without some such structure it would seem logically impossible for any society to exist. Empirically it is only through some of these institutions and roles that the individual can survive, let alone live the moral life, and it is through these alone that many moral, and immoral, practices and actions are made possible. It is, of course, the rules and principles that govern these institutions and roles that are of interest to us in this context, and these have been helpfully distinguished into three categories by differences in the kinds of regulation of behaviour involved.[3]

First, there are those created by institutions of diverse kinds in which the participants have substantial rights and duties of a wide-ranging and sustained character, as for instance the roles of teacher, employer, trade unionist, priest, parent. The regulation here may be to some extent backed by legal regulation, but that is not the form of control here being picked out. It is rather the assumed, implicit, generally understood and accepted demands of the role that is the point, for it is these rather than any legal regulation that determines the character of vast areas of human life. They are there, standing objectively over against the individual, and he will in varying degrees be involved in living within them. Secondly, there are the demands of the legal system, conformity of behaviour to certain rules being enforced by authority. In this case, it is in the main particular types of activity that are prescribed, rather than roles of the kind mentioned in the previous category, though there is no hard and fast boundary between the categories in this respect. Thirdly, there are the generally agreed moral rules and principles of the society to which conformity is expected.

All these categories have forms of sanction attached to them and in the first and third categories there are many forms of public reward. In this public context and its restrictions the individual has necessarily to conduct himself. In many respects the types of behaviour expected may well be rationally defensible, including the sanctions employed. But this will certainly not be the case throughout these structures, and their demands are no doubt in need of constant critical review and challenge as social circumstances change. Many demands may indeed remain for a long period as expressions of thoroughly discredited beliefs and principles. The degree to which the individual can freely conform to these structures will vary, but it is important that their significance in the moral life be appreciated. Human needs of the most basic kind mean that men are interdependent and need an agreed structure for co-operation. It also is the case that their interests can best be safeguarded, in a context where the resources available to individuals are extremely limited, by a high degree of co-operation and specialisation of function. If one adds to this the value of major areas of security and stability in social life for the pursuit of interests that are otherwise unattainable, the value of a public social structure is something all reasonable men must accept. Yet the potential for evil in any such structure can seem almost as great as its potential for good. It needs to be a moral order in all its elements and part of that must be the recognition that public agreement of the three kinds mentioned is necessary or desirable only within limits. Even if freedom is only one fundamental moral principle, it is at the heart of morality, and no society can be morally healthy in which social restrictions extend beyond areas where they are manifestly defensible. The area of private morality is as important for man as that of public morality, because rational autonomy demands it, because the pattern of the public aspects of the good life in our changing context is something we have so far glimpsed very imperfectly and freedom to experiment is needed, and indeed because there may be no one pattern of the good life in its public any more than in its private aspects. Of the possibilities for moral living we still know very little.

But, from another angle, an emphasis on autonomy might seem desirable. Why should not most people, particularly the less intelligent, leave moral decisions to others more able to do the job and be content to accept the advice they are given? A number of points can be made. First, the only person who can judge what ought to be done is not infrequently the person in the actual situation. Many of the highly relevant factors about the circumstances and the people involved, including the agent, may be such that they cannot be known to others. Secondly, it is also the case that new problems are often encountered in which the agent must act immediately without time for advice. Thirdly, it is difficult to see how the making of one person's life by another person can be defended in all but exceptional cases. The subject individual is in a significant degree refusing or not being allowed to exercise certain freedoms. Unless these freedoms are incompatible with the life of reason, why would the restrictions be desirable? In general the life of reason is not only compatible with these freedoms, it would seem to necessitate them. To go back to Peters' fundamental principles, we can only act rationally if we begin from the principle that people ought to be free to determine their actions, and that is a principle not to be countered without good grounds from another principle. If the moral life is the life of reason, then that necessitates my acting in general on a principle of freedom for myself and others to the extent that reason, through other principles, does not run counter to it.

Yet even in these terms can one not argue that some moral judgments do demand superior intelligence and knowledge that ordinary people do not have? That does seem to me to be the case. In most matters of life it is, I think, true that what is necessary to making rational judgments does not require high intelligence, or knowledge that is not available to all. In day-to-day affairs, highly intelligent people are not particularly notable for their high morality, and in so far as they are, it may well be because of the form of education they have received in relevant matters, rather than any innate superiority. Also the qualities needed for the moral life are not simply intellectual, and in these other necessary respects less intelligent people may often be highly gifted. But it is not the case that the rationally autonomous person must himself work out every judgment on every action he ever undertakes, questioning things even to the fundamental principles. He does in fact think things out for himself to the extent that he has the necessary knowledge and abilities. But he recognises when it is in fact rational to seek advice from suitable knowledgeable people, even if that advice should itself be judged by him where it connects with areas on which he is competent. If morality is concerned with the rational life, rational autonomy itself must not be expected or demanded when it is unreasonable to ask for it, either from oneself or others. There will be great diversity in the range of issues on which individuals are capable of judging outside the matters of day-to-day experience. There will be diversity too in the depth of critical questioning and the levels of justification which people can give of the various supposedly moral rules that are common in society. Maybe many are capable of rational judgments over a wide area in terms of questions of fairness, freedom, equality and more localised rules that reflect these principles. Whether or not many could hope to follow the controversial debates of philosophers on the justification of these principles, even if they were presented to them in a suitable form, is another matter. All that rational autonomy in morality demands is as developed a capacity for commitment to making rational judgments as is practically possible under existing conditions and with available methods and resources. To ask more would be unreasonable.[4]

THE CHARACTERISTICS OF MORAL CONSCIOUSNESS

Having argued that the making of autonomous rational judgments about action is the central feature of the moral life, it is perhaps important now to work out in more detail what this demands of the individual.[5] Again, this will be setting out an idea which in individual cases can reasonably be achieved to only a limited degree. In the first place, there are certain intellectual demands. There must be a mastery of the logic of reasoning in general and those distinctive characteristics of moral reasoning in particular which were outlined earlier. This is not a question of a person knowing theoretically what reasoning in this area involves, but of knowing how to so reason, being able to do it, and that does not necessitate a theoretical grasp of the principles involved. In addition, it will be necessary for the fundamental principles to be understood as providing the foundations of the structure of reasons. But if these principles are to be used to make judgments on human situations, they can only operate if they are employed on a great deal of factual knowledge about those situations. For convenience these facts can be put into three categories. There are physical facts about the world and people, say about the properties of drugs, the scarcity of natural resources, or the strength of materials; only in so far as we know the relevant facts and therefore the possible consequences of actions can we use the principles to judge what should be done. But there are also many facts about persons that we also need to know, about ourselves and others concerned. What are their wants and interests, their political or religious beliefs, how do they see situations, what would they feel about the results of possible actions, what would they be likely to do as a result? What are their reasons for what they think? Are they motivated by self-interest rather than wider concerns? Am I myself simply reflecting an established disposition or pattern of emotional response rather than working out a reasoned conclusion as to what to do? Finally, there is a great variety of social or institutional facts that are likely to be relevant. How does this school or family actually function? What principles are at present being used for decisions in this institution and with what justification? What sanctions will operate through public opinion or through the law if certain actions are taken? Of course, one cannot lay down, independently of the problems of action that are to be considered, what areas of knowledge will be necessary to form rational judgments. In areas in which moral judgments are to be taken, however, the person concerned must either already possess the relevant knowledge or have access to it.

The acquisition of the relevant knowledge for any situation and its use in making a judgment may demand many intellectual qualities other than those we immediately associate with reason and knowledge. In particular, the use of the imagination both to conceive alternative situations and to enter into certain types of human relationship may be a condition of acquiring an understanding of others without which a judgment may be seriously ill-informed. Certain types of social skills are equally necessary for actually carrying out in practice moral decisions, for without such executive capacities the decisions will either remain inoperative or be expressed in ways that fail to achieve their intended ends. Unfortunately, we do not begin to have a comprehensive mapping of the qualities needed if a person is to have the forms of intellectual mastery and propositional and procedural knowledge necessary to the making of moral judgments and their effective execution. We can only make the best of the limited and partial understanding we have so far acquired.

But the relevant abilities and types of knowledge provide only the tools and materials for moral actions. The moral life necessitates also a host of personal dispositions. And by a disposition I do not mean merely that a person be such that the probability that something will occur is high, so much as that a settled pattern of thought or behaviour exists in which something will indeed occur unless another disposition takes priority. In this domain of dispositions the moral person must indeed be disposed intellectually to think the issue through, so that he actually makes the moral judgments for which he is equipped, and also disposed to extend the range and depth of his judgments as is reasonable in given circumstances. What is more, if the morally right action is to occur the person must be disposed to act on his moral judgments. To refer to these dispositions to think and to act in this way must not mislead us into thinking that there are in fact just two simple qualities here. To be disposed to think out one's moral position, even when it is appropriate to do so, may depend on a vast variety of factors. We may be so disposed in some contexts, but not in others; on, say, matters of sexual relations, yet not on matters of relations with one's subordinates at work. How far the disposition to think out what to do, or for that matter to act on the result of such thought, is situation-dependent is a matter of some dispute, but it is readily understandable that many factors might well make it so. When a person does in fact act in ways that are clearly the result of particular types of moral judgment, we invoke the labels of virtues and vices. A person is honest or dishonest, courageous or cowardly, truthful or a liar, by virtue of just the kind of dispositions to think and act that I am concerned with. Certainly in these cases the very existence of many different virtues and vices would lead one to think that there are in fact many distinct personal qualities here which frequently occur in varied combinations in the individual. There is perhaps too a hierarchy of these dispositions, for some are more specific than others, the general seeming to include the particular. It is one thing to be punctual, it is another to be conscientious. Yet whether or not a general trait of conscientiousness exists rather than a number of similar but distinct traits is a matter for empirical evidence. The achievement of the moral life at all would, however, seem to depend on certain dispositions for which we have general labels, whatever psychological realities they may cover. It is hard to see how anyone could act morally in any area of life where a disposition to act on an intellectual judgment was not in appropriate cases stronger than a disposition or inclination to pursue the instant gratification of one's own personal desires. Strength of will, or persistence in difficult circumstances of all kinds, and integrity are both expressions of characteristics that are of the essence of moral living. Yet again we must be realistic about the empirical facts about these qualities and not assume a simpler structure to them than is justifiable from the evidence. The transfer of dispositions is in principle just as elusive and deceptive a doctrine as the transfer of abilities in intellectual matters.[6]

But the place of dispositions in the moral life extends well beyond the areas so far considered. In addition to dispositions to make rational judgments and to act on them, there must also be dispositions to act in accordance with rationally defensible rules and principles on those many occasions when deliberation is either impossible or unnecessary. If, as was argued, rational autonomy does not, because it cannot, demand deliberation during a great deal of life, morality must to a significant degree consist of dispositions simply to act according to the appropriate rules and principles. To a great extent this will mean the agent is fully conscious of what he is doing, but he does it spontaneously without reasoning out why he should do this, it being the case that, were he challenged, he could justify the action, granted he had the necessary ability and knowledge. But for the fully consistent moral life, the dispositions must also be such that even totally unconscious behaviour is in keeping with the same rules and principles. It would in fact seem to be the case that what we usually mean by a virtue or a vice (say, honesty or cruelty) is not simply the disposition to think and act in a certain manner after deliberation, but also to act so spontaneously and even unconsciously. The dispositions of the moral life therefore need to be all of a piece and consistently related to the person's underlying moral rules and principles. They must, however, never be so determined that they cannot be examined critically by the agent and steps taken for their modification whenever this is judged appropriate and desirable.

All of a piece too with the person's moral beliefs must be his emotional responses, the third area in which the moral life is expressed.[7] As was mentioned earlier in discussing the emotive theory in ethics, there is one sense in which all emotions are necessarily tied to beliefs, for what makes an emotional experience what it is is dependent on some understanding, appraisal, or belief about the significance of the situation for the person himself. To fear, hate, or love is only possible as a result of some self-referring grasp of the state of affairs. In the harmonious moral life, a person loves those things that are morally right and good, that are on rational grounds justifiable; he fears those things that are in fact a threat or danger and so on. In practice, however, the situation is usually very much more complicated. A person's beliefs about many situations may be simply false—for instance, based on mistaken stereotypes of the ideas and behaviour of people from other social classes or other countries. The self-referring element in the belief about a situation may involve quite unjustifiable moral principles as to what ought to be done. But, yet more significantly, a person's emotional responses are all too often tied to forms of judgment of situations that are not only unjustifiable, but are also deep-seated, well-established patterns of belief. It is manifestly the case that emotional response is not infrequently the outcome of certain dispositions to believe what in fact we know to be irrational or unreasonable.

But assuming it were possible for a person's moral emotions to be based entirely on rational moral judgments, is the achievement of such a pattern of emotional life necessary or even desirable? Provided a persons's actions are morally appropriate, is not the demand for certain patterns of emotional response asking too much? Indeed, are emotional experiences themselves of any moral significance? Is it not true that the person's beliefs and dispositions constitute the whole of the story about the individual that is relevant? Are emotions not an irrelevant flotsam on the surface of those aspects of the person that really matter? We do not, I think, at present know the answers to these questions. But three relevant points can perhaps be made.

First, the existence of emotional responses is a very effective indication of the existence within the person of certain beliefs or attitudes. The significance of these dispositions to judge in certain ways, their force and power within the individual's life, should not be ignored. The occurrence of feelings of disgust or hate in inappropriate situations indicates the existence of dispositions to think and perhaps also to act in an immoral way. As indicators of one's moral character, and the possible outcome of that character in action, emotions ought therefore not to be underestimated. Secondly, as forms of experience to which people are subject, they are sources of pain or pleasure, delight or distress, and as such may be in themselves therefore morally desirable or undesirable. In so far as certain beliefs and actions are or are not justifiable, the occurrence of a pleasurable or painful emotion as an accompanying state of mind may well itself be an additional good or evil. That the unnecessary suffering of oneself or others can hardly be regarded as morally desirable is a further morally significant factor, as too are the simple facts that emotional states occupy a person's time and energy to the exclusion of other things and can positively interfere with other mental events for good or ill. This leads to the third point, that the very occurrence of these states of pleasure or pain can itself become a reason in determining what ought to be done. If, for instance, a particular action has caused a feeling of remorse, that feeling can function as an inner determining sanction similar to the outer sanctions of punishment. The character of this sanction will be commented on further when the nature of conscience is discussed. At this point, however, perhaps it might be noted that there is a positive as well as a negative parallel to be drawn between inner and outer sanctions. The satisfaction or pleasure that can come from doing what is good or desirable may be just as powerful a force in moral action as the pain of the punishment for doing what is judged wrong. The whole effectiveness of this mechanism rests, of course, on the gaps that can exist between certain forms of judgment to which we may be disposed, the judgments we consciously hold that are subject to modification, and the actions we actually perform.

THE MORAL LIFE AND THE SECULAR CHRISTIAN

The preceding characterisation of the elements of the moral life has in fact been given in terms which find little or no place in traditional Christian accounts. In particular, it has made no use of specifically Christian concepts. To that extent it has been a thoroughly secular picture. Yet the account must not on that score be interpreted as necessarily inconsistent with certain forms of Christian belief. Much Biblical description of moral experience, though not employing such categories as 'disposition', 'skill', 'emotion', 'institution' or 'role', could readily be expressed within these without any particular injustice. Yet these newer concepts are usually associated with a certain general theory of the nature of mind and its attributes which is not that presupposed in much traditional Christian teaching. Important though the differences are, too much must not be made of them, however, for an intelligent approach to Christian belief seems to me not to necessitate the particular account of mind with which it is most commonly associated.

In crude terms, Christians tend to think of the mind as consisting primarily of a number of distinct naturally-given mental organs which carry out particular functions. First, there is reason, by means of which we think logically, but which sometimes works inaccurately, sometimes operates inappropriately, is sometimes interfered with by human desires. There are then the natural desires, a whole range of given lusts, tendencies, wants, which in many circumstances constitute temptations to do wrong. They are both feelings and dispositions to behave in certain ways. Conscience is the element of mind that is the source of man's moral awareness, a combination of feeling and understanding. Again, like reason, it may be tainted in its operation, but nevertheless it has within it the seeds of genuine moral insight. Finally, there is the will, man's uncertain capacity to carry out whatever he decides to do. In these terms man's moral failures can be seen as the product of numerous human weaknesses. Reason may operate defectively; the natural desires, which are necessarily self-orientated, may override all else; the conscience may be warped or silenced; the will may be lacking in strength and therefore ineffective. The natural corruption of the person is to be seen in these inadequacies which mar the whole of natural moral life. It is therefore only by supernatural aid that the effects of these weaknesses can be overcome and the moral life be satisfactorily lived.

The elements in the account of mind I developed earlier differ from those in this traditional picture in two major respects.[8] To begin with, the various aspects of mind are not taken to be distinct mental organs that operate in specifically determined ways. There are not thought to be any such entities as the reason or the conscience. A person does not possess a will. That people do reason, make judgments, feel guilt, behave persistently in face of opposition and so on, is not disputed, but it is no longer assumed that there is some one psychological entity that, according to its nature, produces these results in each case. The source of these results may be far more complex than, and the organisation of mental operations very different from, that which these traditional categories imply. The phenomena that are being accounted for are not being questioned; it is the mechanistic model of mental organs or muscles as their source that is considered quite unnecessary. We need to approach the phenomena without traditional presuppositions, and if we do that, very different types of explanation of them begin to emerge.

But further, the notion that these aspects of the mind have the features that they customarily display simply because of their natural constitution is no longer acceptable. There is very good reason indeed to think that patterns of reasoning are in major respects not innate but learnt in society. True, there must be a natural capacity to learn, but what is learnt can vary greatly, and the structure of forms of accurate argument is one such outcome of learning. Any individual entirely on his own could achieve little in this direction from natural endowment; it is only by learning within a society patterns of argument slowly developed over successive generations that we have our present forms of reasoning. So too dispositions to feel guilt no doubt have a natural root, but what we feel guilty about, the pattern of conscience that we have, would seem to be a social product, not an inbuilt moral voice. The whole structure of mental functioning must therefore be looked at, not as a product from within so much as acquired, taken on board, from without. Errors, inadequacies and inappropriateness within the pattern of functioning in the mind can thus be examined to see how such forms of functioning were acquired. When one aspect of mind, say the emotions, or desires, interferes with another, say the working out of a moral argument, that confusion can be seen not as an inevitable natural corruption in man but the result of learnt dispositions.

The force of these two emphases in our contemporary understanding of the nature of mind can perhaps best be seen by looking briefly at the way what were once thought to be the activities of conscience now tend to be viewed.[9] To start with, what were considered expressions of conscience can be seen to cover both cognitive judgments as to what is morally right or wrong and also states of emotional response to situations. It is the intuitive form of cognitive judgment, not the outcome of deliberation, that was thought to be the voice of conscience in indicating moral truth, and feelings of guilt were seen as the appropriate result of acting against such judgment. But the two are quite distinct activities of mind, not necessarily related together as this picture implies. Emotional responses are tied to judgments, but not necessarily to those that are operating in intuitive cognitive judgments of which we are consciously aware. In any given case, these judgments may be very different, and both of these may be different again from carefully considered judgments. In this situation, which of the three is to be taken as representing what is morally defensible is of some importance, and it is difficult to see how in general anything other than the considered judgment can be accorded that status. Studies in variations in intuitive judgments and in guilt feelings indicate considerable variations between cultural groups and between individuals within groups. The evidence that these result from differences in learning tells heavily against any theory of a natural inbuilt voice that accurately expresses, either cognitively or emotionally, an absolute right or wrong. There are strong indications too of social factors that determine what is learnt and thus incorporated into these two aspects of conscience, probably through forms of conditioning by reward and punishment in early childhood and patterns of introjection and identification. It can be seen from these comments that the existence of what we refer to as conscience is not in any sense here in question, but the way we interpret the facts and see their significance in the moral life can no longer be simply along traditional Christian lines.

What has been said of conscience and its character could be paralleled in an analysis of the desires or the will. The elements of the moral life that are distinguished in traditional Christian teaching are thus the result of tying together different features of that life we would now regard as more helpfully kept distinct. To unite certain types of judgment and emotion under conscience only serves to hide their important complexities. But such unities can also mistakenly suggest that the elements are innate, as when certain dispositions and emotions are conceived as lusts and desires. How far they are innate and how far learnt ought not to be prejudged. Unities can also imply a single source for elements of the moral life when none exists. To group even a set of similar dispositions under the will can misleadingly hide diversities in their acquisition and in their context-related operation. That we have psychological elements that are what they are in particular character as a result of learning, and therefore as a result of factors over which we might come to have significant control, is crucial to our hopes for moral education. To attribute moral inadequacies to inbuilt natural defects, be these flaws in moral understanding through a corrupted conscience, or flaws in moral living through weakness of will and corrupt desires, is too quick a move. Manifestly learning to judge intuitively in a morally principled way is a major undertaking about which we as yet know little, but if it is indeed learnt, maybe we can hope to do something about it. And the same goes for the dispositions of strength of will, or the development of morally appropriate desires.

But what then is the secular Christian to make of the demands of the moral life? If moral failings have a natural explanation, and they can, in principle, be naturally prevented, what then has Christian belief to say about moral living? Just as in the question of moral justification I argued it was a mistake to think of Christian belief supplying justifications we otherwise lack, so it seems to me it is also a mistake to think of Christian faith as providing an extra element to the mechanisms of the moral life which is missing on a purely natural approach. Christians must, I think, reconcile themselves fully to the truth that men can naturally do morally good actions, and that they can live the moral life without the injection into that life of divine, supernatural force, as something over and above the natural operations of the mind that I have sought to characterise. There is thus a fully natural description of moral living with no gaps within it needing to be filled by notions of spiritual aid. The religious account of the moral life must then be seen as describing that life at another level, concerned with its ultimate metaphysical underpinning, its ultimate source and character, the ultimate dynamics of elements that are operational, but only through the naturally constituted mechanisms. At this level, the notion of supernatural support or aid as universally necessary to every morally good action is a claim that must be judged seriously as a religious insight. What it cannot be taken to mean is that such support or aid is something that must somehow be added to the natural processes of the moral life. The living of the moral life is, in principle, something we can ourselves do and do directly. If we do that, then we are thereby living the Christian life in its moral aspects. To reverse the order, and think that by living the Christian life we can thereby live the moral life, is precisely to mistake the level of our operations as human beings and to misconceive what the religious life must presuppose. The moral life does not presuppose the Christian life, it is rather that the Christian life presupposes the moral. It is true that metaphysically the moral life is underpinned by the realities of which the religious understanding of life speaks, but our way into the religious life in thought and deliberate action can only be through the natural moral life.

F

Men can only come to live the moral life if they attend to the natural elements of it. If we endlessly invoke religious ways of by-passing that immediate responsibility, religion stands in the way of morality, it does not promote it. Moral living will come by our being assiduously secular in our approach to all its complexities. Once more the secular Christian is on all fours with the rational non-Christian, for in the rational moral life there is nothing contrary to the Christian life, the former is indeed the vehicle of the latter. What we cannot do in the actual business of living is successfully attend to morality by getting at it from the religious, metaphysical end. Christians like all others can get at it only from the natural end, by taking it for what it is.

Yet surely there is more to the significance of religion for the moral life than this. To say that one can best live the Christian life by attending to moral matters in a totally secular fashion, developing one's capacities and dispositions without any religious reference, seems completely reductionist. But there are two particular respects in which such reductionism is not being embraced in this approach. First, the acceptance of Christian teaching leads to certain elements of living which are specifically religious in character and which necessarily enter the over-all life-style of the person. Particular beliefs and dispositions to act in religious affairs, patterns of emotional responses in, say, worship, and the living of roles within religious institutions, all constitute elements in the Christian's life that the non-Christian will not share. They necessarily exist within the total complex of beliefs, dispositions, emotions and roles of the individual life. In this sense, though no distinctive spiritual mechanisms are being invoked, the moral life is in this case infused with a distinctly Christian element in all its aspects and may clearly take on a distinctive character in particular overt activities. But even here one must be careful to recognise the necessary harmony of all such distinctively Christian elements with rational morality, if the proper relationship of the secular and the religious is to be retained. And that, because of the status of all metaphysical and religious claims, means the placing of the distinctively Christian elements in those areas of life which rational secular concerns leave open-ended.

This means that where public aspects of the moral life are concerned these elements cannot be properly determinative and this is again to accept the appropriateness of the 'privatisation' of the distinctive features of Christian morality. Nevertheless, for the life-style of the individual, the existence of these elements may be highly significant.

The second feature distinctive of the Christian life is simply that religious beliefs about the moral life as a whole can engender a strata of beliefs, dispositions and emotions that supervene on moral beliefs, dispositions, emotions and roles. They constitute psychologically a further level of personal involvement that presupposes the level of moral involvement. Again, no further mechanism of the mind is being postulated, it is a further particular content that is informing the processes of the mind. On the secular Christian view it is here that the focus of so much Christian teaching on the living of the moral life in general must be found. It is in the additional emphasis that religion brings to the development of appropriate moral aspects of the personal life, by seeing them within beliefs, dispositions and emotions of a wider and metaphysically more ultimate nature, that the religious impact on morality is centred. It is in this way that the significance of prayer and grace may properly be seen to operate and that all moral acts can come to be seen as not my own acts but as the actions of 'Christ living within me.'

References

1 See WILSON, J., WILLIAMS, N., SUGARMAN, B. (1967). *Introduction to Moral Education*. Harmondsworth: Penguin Books. Chapter 1.
2 For discussion of the relationship between autonomy and authenticity, see papers by PETERS, R. S. and FEINBERG, J. (1973). In Doyle, J. F. (ed.), *Educational Judgments*. London: Routledge and Kegan Paul.
3 I am here using a classification in BAIER, K. (1971). 'Ethical Pluralism and Moral Education'. In Beck, C. M., Crittenden, B. S., Sullivan, E. V. (eds.), *Moral Education*. Toronto: University of Toronto Press.
4 For a fuller discussion of the nature of autonomy and its place in the moral life, see:
   BAIER, K. (1973). 'Moral Autonomy as an aim of Moral Education.' In Langford, G. and O'Connor, D. J. (eds.), *New Essays in the Philosophy of Education*. London: Routledge and Kegan Paul.
5 For an alternative outline of these demands, see the characterisation in WILSON, J. (1973). *The Assessment of Morality*. Slough: N.F.E.R.; and in WILSON, J., WILLIAMS, N., SUGARMAN, B. (1967). *Introduction to Moral Education*. Harmondsworth: Penguin Books.
6 A most helpful summary of the present state of psychological research into this and many other aspects of the moral life will be found in: WRIGHT, D. (1971). *The Psychology of Moral Behaviour*. Harmondsworth: Pengnuin Books.
7 For a fuller discussion of the nature of emotions, see:
   DEARDEN, R. F., HIRST, P. H., PETERS, R. S. (eds.) (1972). *Education and the Development of Reason*. London: Routledge and Kegan Paul. Part 2.
   See also PETERS, R. S. (1973). *Reason and Compassion*. London: Routledge and Kegan Paul.
8 The most influential critical treatment of the traditional view of mind is that in a book now regarded as a philosophical classic:
   RYLE, G. (1949). *The Concept of Mind*. London: Hutchinson.

9   The concept of conscience has been discussed in a number of recent papers. See:
BAIER, K. (1973). 'Moral Autonomy as an aim of Moral Education.' In Langford, G. and O'Connor, J. D. (eds.), *New Essays in the Philosophy of Education*. London: Routledge and Kegan Paul.

WILLIAMS, N. and WILLIAMS, S. (1970). *The Moral Development of Children*. London: Macmillan.

ARONFREED, J. (1971). 'Some problems for a theory of the acquisition of conscience'. In Beck, C. M., Crittenden, B. S., Sullivan, E. V. (eds.), *Moral Education*. Toronto: University of Toronto Press.

CHAPTER 5

The Secularisation of Education

EDUCATION: CHRISTIAN OR SECULAR?

Having endeavoured to characterise as far as I think one can the general features of the moral life in a way that does justice to the demands of secularisation, yet seeks not to prejudge many highly important religious considerations, I have thereby implicitly given a picture of the aims of moral education as I see it. But that characterisation has concentrated entirely on the nature of morality and not at all on the nature of education. It has therefore left unclear the significance of these elements of morality as aims within education. If one turns then to look at the nature of education so as to clarify in what ways the elements of the moral life are related to it, it must be recognised from the start, I think, that our notion of education has itself undergone a transformation which is an expression of secularisation just as much as our notion of morality.[1] In particular, there has now emerged in our society a concept of education which makes the whole idea of Christian education a kind of nonsense. From this point of view, the idea that there is a characteristically or distinctively Christian form of education seems just as much a mistake as the idea that there is a distinctively Christian form of mathematics, of engineering, or of farming. In mathematics, engineering and farming we have developed activities in which what is right or wrong, or good or bad, of its kind, is determined by rational principles which make the activity what it is. Mathematical proofs must be judged right or wrong according to the principles of mathematical reasoning. A bridge to stay up in a gale must be designed strictly according to the principles of engineering. And the principles that govern these matters of mathematics, engineering and farming are neither Christian nor non-Christian, neither for nor against Christianity. Nor is anything in these areas decided properly by appeal to Christian tradition, the Christian Scriptures or anything else of that kind.

Once, of course, this was not so. Man's view of the physical world and how to cope with it in practical affairs was at least in part determined by his religious beliefs. It was not thought possible to attain the relevant knowledge on autonomous, independent, rational grounds. But the pursuits I have mentioned have now been recognised as legitimately autonomous, and an exactly similar status is, I suggest, quite properly coming to be accorded to education as a whole. Here too we are progressively coming to understand that the issues must be settled independently of any questions of religious beliefs.

What exactly is wrong with the idea of Christian education is not easy to disentangle. Much of what one is offered under this label is in fact very dubious both from an educational and indeed from a Christian point of view. Usually it is based on very general moral principles, backed by perhaps Scripture or Christian tradition, which, having little or no explicit educational content, are then applied to educational problems in a highly debatable way. Questions about curricula, discipline, teaching methods are often baldly asserted as Christian on such flimsy grounds. But clearly, the general moral principles that people use to back up these beliefs about education do not alone determine any particular, practically relevant, educational principles. To get these, one must consider equally important matters of psychological and sociological fact, the structure of our social institutions, the availability of money and manpower, and so on. All these and many other considerations must enter into the discussion before one can move from very general principles of a moral kind to specific educational recommendations, and it is on just these particular considerations that ideas of so-called Christian education are often quite indefensible. The main point to be noted, however, is that none of these other considerations has anything to do with Christian beliefs. What is more, it seems to me that the general principles on which the whole exercise is based are usually not in any sense significantly Christian either, though people might appeal to Christian texts, or Christian tradition, in support of them. Working from this end, from general moral principles, I suggest that one simply cannot produce anything that is in any significant sense a distinctive Christian view of education.

But if one tries to work from the other end, formulating educational principles from what is specifically said in Scripture about education, one seems to run into an equally impossible situation. If you take what the Bible says about punishment and discipline, and try to compose some general educational principle from this, you will not, I think, get very far. To take ideas of social control out of a Biblical social context and transfer them directly to an East End school in our twentieth-century industrial society is patently ludicrous. Christians of any intelligence have long since recognised the need to disentangle within Biblical teaching the general principles that can be legitimately applied to our own context and the practices justifiable only in the social and cultural circumstances of Biblical times. The problem then is how to abstract the principles without entering on inconclusive debate about Biblical interpretation. If that hurdle is surmounted, is one likely to achieve much that is both educationally significant and distinctively Christian? I think not. And even if one does get so far, how much agreement can there be amongst Christians on particular applications of these principles? Experience suggests very little, if any. On these grounds, I suggest that a distinctive Biblical or Christian view of education simply is not discoverable. One just cannot produce anything of substance that deserves to be so labelled.

It might be said in reply, however, that I have spoilt my case by vastly overstating it. If we cannot get an all-embracing view of Christian education, surely there are some things in education on which Christians and non-Christians would disagree. If so, does it not follow that there is in part a distinctively Christian concept of education, one which is distinguishable from other views at least in these particular areas if not in others? If one cannot get everything necessary for educational practice from Christian teaching, surely one can get something, and something distinctive. The Christian will, for instance, surely want his children brought up in the Christian faith, and that the non-Christian will certainly not want. In this respect at least their ideas of the content of education will be radically different. Yet another Christian may well say that the last thing one should do, as part of education, is bring up a child in any faith, even the Christian faith. This second Christian would maintain that communicating an understanding of the Christian faith is a legitimate part of education, and with that many non-Christians in our society might well agree, but bringing up a child within any particular faith is not what education is about. What we have here are two quite different views of education. According to the first, it is concerned with passing on to children what we believe, so that they in turn come to believe it to be true. According to the second view, education should not be determined by what any group simply believes, but by what on publicly

acknowledged rational grounds we can claim to know and understand.

The first of these concepts of education I shall call the primitive
concept, for it clearly expresses the view of education a primitive
tribe might have when it seeks to pass on to the next generation its
rituals, its way of farming and so on, according to its own customs
and beliefs. Whatever is held by the group to be true or valuable,
simply because it is held to be true or valuable, is what is passed on
so that it comes to be held as true and valuable by others in their turn.
On this view, clearly there can be a Christian concept of education,
one based on what Christians hold to be true and valuable in education, according to which Christians seek that the next generation
shall think likewise. Similarly there can be a Humanist or a Buddhist
concept; indeed, there will be as many concepts of education as there
are systems of beliefs and values, concepts overlapping in character
in so far as the beliefs and values of the different groups overlap.

The second view of education is much more sophisticated, arising
from a recognition that not all the things held to be true or valuable
by a group are of the same status. Some of their claims and activities
will be rationally defensible on objective grounds, whereas others,
perhaps held equally tenaciously, may on objective grounds be highly
debatable. Some may in fact be matters of nothing but mere custom
and tradition. Once it is fully recognised that the belief that something
is true, even if that belief is universal, does not of itself make it true,
a new principle emerges for carefully assessing what we pass on to
others and how we wish them to regard it. That we hold something
to be true or valuable is of itself no reason why anyone else should so
regard it. That something can, on the appropriate objective grounds,
be shown to be true or reasonable is a very good reason for passing
it on to others. But even then what we must surely seek is that they
will hold it, not because we hold it, but because there are objective
grounds. Only then will they be prepared to reconsider, and where
necessary revise, their beliefs and practices when new evidence and
better arguments arise.

The second, sophisticated view of education is thus concerned with
passing on beliefs and practices according to, and together with, their
objective status. It is dominated by a concern for knowledge, for
truth, for reasons, distinguishing these clearly from mere belief, con-
jecture and subjective preference. On this view, when science is
taught, its methods and procedures are seen to be as important as
any contemporary scientific beliefs, for these may in significant

respects have to be changed. In history, pupils are introduced to examining evidence, so that they come to recognise that claims about what happened must satisfy the canons of historical scholarship. Where there is dispute, debate and divergence of opinion, this fact is taught. Where in any area there do not seem to be agreed objective principles of judgment, exactly that is what is taught. Of course, mistakes will be made in seeking to follow as closely as possible the ideals of objectivity and reason, but education committed to these ends will be very different from education determined by the particular beliefs and values of a limited group.

On this second view, the character of education is not settled by any appeal to Christian, Humanist or Buddhist beliefs. Such an appeal is illegitimate, for the basis is logically more fundamental, being found in the canons of objectivity and reason, canons against which Christian, Humanist and Buddhist beliefs must, in their turn and in the appropriate way, be assessed. When the domain of religious beliefs is so manifestly one in which there are at present no clearly recognisable objective grounds for judging claims, to base education on any such claims would be to forsake the pursuit of objectivity, however firm our commitment might be to any one set of such beliefs. Indeed, an education based on a concern for objectivity and reason, far from allying itself with any specific religious claims, must involve teaching the radically controversial character of all such claims. An understanding of religious claims it can perfectly well aim at, but commitment to any one set, in the interests of objectivity, it cannot either assume or pursue.

The concern for reason and objectivity which dominates this concept of education is clearly directed to the development of people who are rational, autonomous beings in every area of life. Up to this point I have deliberately not referred specifically to the moral elements in such an education, but I trust it is patently clear that it involves developing precisely the characteristics with which I was concerned earlier. The major objections to this concept, as can be imagined, all attempt to deny the autonomy of the very developments education seeks, be these in, say, morality, the sciences, history, the arts, or mathematics. In some or all of these areas it is maintained that one is necessarily involved in presuppositions of a religious nature. On moral matters I have said enough already. In what way mathematics is supposed to depend on Christian principles when its concepts and forms of argument are so totally devoid of religious reference, it is hard to see. As I argued earlier, what is meant by saying that science rests on Christian presuppositions, when the tests for its claims are ultimately matters of sense observation, is obscure. Scientific terms have meaning and criteria of application which are not connected with religious concepts of any sort. They are in this sense autonomous, and scientific understanding is therefore of its nature autonomous. To maintain that it was only in a context of Christian belief that science did in fact arise, even if true, does not affect the nature of the activity of science at all. The pursuit is perfectly compatible with quite other beliefs, as is obvious in the present day, and nothing by way of historical, sociological, or psychological analysis can in any way deny the claim that the concepts and principles of science are in no sense logically connected with Christian beliefs. That there is here an autonomous domain of knowledge and understanding seems to me indisputable. And surely this is why what matters in science, as in any other pursuit, is the mastery of its own logical and methodological principles, not holding any particular religious beliefs.

But it might be objected that, if science is autonomous, historical studies are not, for an understanding of, say, the Reformation must be either Catholic or Protestant. Yet surely even this is an unacceptable claim if it is intended to deny the objectivity of contemporary historical scholarship. What matters is truth based on evidence, irrespective of the particular religious beliefs of the scholar. It is justice to the historical data that counts and possible interpretive bias is itself a matter of objective recognition. The idea of coming to a situation to interpret it from a set of religious beliefs to which one personally subscribes is to reject the demand of historical scholarship. What is true of historical studies is, I suggest, also true of literary and even religious studies. I see no reason why there should not be, and indeed there is already being practised, an objective study of religions in which the particular religious beliefs of students are an irrelevant consideration. To understand beliefs or actions does not necessitate that one either accepts or approves of them, and to teach for such an understanding demands acceptance or approval of them by neither teacher nor pupil.

But even if the autonomy thesis is accepted, and it is granted that something called education could be planned and conducted in terms of the second sophisticated concept that I outlined, it might still be argued that this would be undesirable. If education can be understood in two senses, either in the primitive sense of simply passing on beliefs and practices or in the sophisticated sense of passing on knowledge and understanding and reason, why should we not stick to the first which can take on a distinctively Christian form?

The more primitive concept exerts a peculiar fascination, because in certain important respects it seems inescapable. How can we help but pass on the beliefs and values that we have, for even to develop reason is to do just that? In one sense this is so, but to regard the handing on of reason as the handing on of values and beliefs we simply agree on is to mistake the significance of reason and its connection with objectivity. It is just because of this distinction in our beliefs and the limits reason sets to education that the second concept has arisen. We can escape merely passing on our values and beliefs by passing on as far as is reasonable the most fundamental capacities to challenge those values and beliefs and by not presenting them as having a status that is not defensible. But is that not an attitude possible only for the education of an elite? To which the answer must be surely no, as the principle of such education is to be applied reasonably, and no man should expect to call in question matters quite beyond his present knowledge and competence and his having reasonable grounds for doubt. But is this approach not to suggest that we cannot pass on any firm content in such matters as morals, religion, literature, history, or even science? Again, the answer must be no. Where there exist grounds for judgments and no good grounds for calling matters in question, we have no reason to refrain from teaching such elements as what they are, the truth and defensible judgments in so far as we have achieved them. The development of autonomy in any area does not mean the making of purely subjective decisions, nor the acceptance of principles of judgment without accepting any content of conclusions. But what of the excessive intellectualism of such a concept of education? Is it not an excessively partial and limited notion when there is so much more to a person than the activities of reason? To which the answer is that this concept of education is concerned with the development of the person in every aspect, be this intellect, dispositions, emotions, roles, skills. The point is that the person should develop in all aspects in ways that constitute a rationally autonomous life. The development of the person's reason is therefore central in all areas, but no more the whole story in any other area of life than it was shown to be in morality. The concept that is being defended aims at a type of person and nothing less than that. He is to have the dispositions, emotions, skills and so on appropriate to a life of reason with all the substantive commitments that must involve. Education itself involves a commitment to reason on the part of the educator, no more and no less. Looked at this way, it is hard to see how any concept of education that seeks for more than this, be it in beliefs, dispositions, or any other aspect of personal development, could ever be defended, even if we have to admit that much of what goes on in the name of education may be seeking inappropriate forms of commitment and response.

It is built into education on these terms that, on matters of controversy on which public agreement is not necessary, for instance on some issues in religion and the arts, the private decisions of individuals must be respected. The limits of education can there legitimately go no further than reason itself determines. Understanding of different opinions, dispositions and ways of life is certainly included. The development of any aspects of the person that presuppose any beliefs or judgments beyond those that are rationally defensible can, however, have no place. How to draw that line in practice is far from easy, but the principle is surely clear. In religion, education can certainly include understanding a faith, and this in turn might involve imaginatively entering into the activities of ritual and worship which are essential to that religion. What cannot be part of education, however, would be seeking to develop, say, a disposition to worship in that faith, or certain emotions of love of God, when that very disposition, or these emotions, are only a justifiable development if the religion is accepted by the individual. That acceptance I have argued is a personal, private judgment which education, committed to reason alone as it is, has no right to foreclose.[2]

EDUCATION WITHIN THE LIMITS OF REASON

If education must thus respect the limits of reason and nevertheless aim at developing the rational, autonomous person, it must, at least in principle, attend to development in all those domains of reason that man has achieved. Though there must again be a rational application of the principle, education must prima facie be concerned with an appropriate level of autonomy in all the distinct types of reason. I have argued elsewhere that there would seem to be some seven areas in which serious claims to a distinct type of understanding and thought must be recognised.[3] These are the domains of the understanding of formal logical relations, of the physical world, of persons, in moral judgments, in the arts, in religion and in philosophy. But again, it must be emphasised that in any such area the rationally autonomous person must acquire more than an intellectual grasp. Each area involves distinctive dispositions, emotions, skills, roles, and the desired achievements for any given individual in any one area must depend on a multiplicity of factors that will in some major respects be unique. A person can only develop into an autonomous being in ways, and to a degree, that are reasonable in relation to the practical limitations of his personal context. What we must not do, any more than we can possibly help, is irrationally determine a person's development, even when our eyes are on his autonomy, by restricting his abilities, dispositions, skill and so on without good cause. Across all areas and within each area all forms of rationally defensible achievement must be in principle open to everyone. The maximum rational autonomy of the individual that is reasonable in his circumstances must be our basic concern. It is only too obvious that our social structure, the organisation and curricula of our schools, not to mention the influences of many other institutions and forces in our society, restrict the autonomy of individuals in respect of both the areas in which they are capable of effectively operating at all and the level of that operation within these areas. Be it in job choice, leisure pursuits, religious adherence, or even sexual orientation, we are still determining people in ways that irrationally reduce their autonomy. What is more, we are doing this not only through the multitudinous implicit pressures within our institutions which are not concerned directly with the development of individuals. We are doing it too in our schools and other institutions which are explicitly planned to promote education. We are still too primitive in our concept of education, too much concerned with the preservation of the past and the present, too little concerned with what in the end alone can be justified, developing the rational, autonomous life.

This account of a secularised concept of autonomous education, which is committed to reason and nothing beyond that, is in no sense anti-religious. Indeed, it seems to me it is precisely the concept of education an intelligent Christian must accept, just as he must accept the autonomy of moral judgments and of the moral life. It is one in which the substantive achievements in all areas of understanding are taken as a firm content for education whilst presenting the underlying rational basis to that content and the principles of reasoning in each area as a means for constant critical questioning. Nothing, not even the critical principles themselves, are regarded as beyond such questioning. In all areas the rational status of man's understanding must be as truthfully reflected as possible. In religion, I have argued, this means that no particular substantive religious claims can be either assumed to be, or simply taught as, objectively acceptable. Their radically controversial character must be recognised. In that case, no practical principles that derive entirely from religious claims can be either assumed to be right or instructed in. Nor can any distinctively religious backing to moral claims be regarded as more than controversial. All of which is to say that religion is seen as a private matter on which education can help the individual as far as objective considerations permit, but on which it has nothing further to say. Objective understanding of religion in all its aspects, including an understanding of 'religious morality', is part of education. But the cultivation of dispositions to use one set of religious concepts, or indeed any, dispositions to practise a religion, religiously rooted emotions, and the acceptance of any religious roles, all these are outside religious education in this secular sense.

Where morality itself is concerned, the position is very different. The activity of education involves decisions, roles and personal relationships that are based on moral principles. If there were no significant body of rationally defensible principles, there would have to be some way of agreeing on certain rules for education to occur at all. If moral education for maximum defensible autonomy were attempted with such conventional agreement recognised as the basis of its principles, an inherently unstable situation would be being promoted, as no ultimately objective grounds for deciding issues one way rather than another are even being sought. Nevertheless, that would be education in my second defensible sense and a form of rational pragmatism. Many would take this position and, of course, some of the important things I have said about morality would apply to it.

If, however, as I have argued, there exists a body of substantive principles and basic rules that can be objectively justified for our society, even if in certain areas of life we still cannot reach any rational conclusions, moral education takes on a very different look. Where these principles and rules are concerned there is every reason to proceed as in, say, the teaching of science, mathematics, or history. There is a body of understanding and its justification, plus principles for criticism, that provides a content for the development of rational dispositions to think and to act, for appropriate emotional development, and for justifiable role training. The development of capacities and dispositions to critically reassess the substantive body of understanding, related dispositions, emotions and roles in this education is

extremely important, but not only at that formal level of criticism
does moral education have a specific content. At the first order level
of moral action too a quite determinable defensible content is available. In so far as principles and rules for action lack rational justification, moral education lacks this objective ground on which to
commit itself to the development of belief and the appropriate first
order dispositions. Where in public affairs and in education agreement is nevertheless necessary, we are unavoidably thrown back on
other procedures, taking what is generally accepted as the basis in
the way I instanced previously. As I then suggested, in this area moral
education for autonomy will be unstable in its achievements, but
nevertheless it is what we should aim at. To the extent that rational
justification is lacking and public agreement on principles and rules
for action is not necessary, moral education can properly concern
itself only with those matters that will appropriately help the individual to make a private judgment. There are thus in principle three
different levels of principles and rules which moral education must
recognise: those for which we have every reason to think there is
rational justification, those for which there is no such justification
but on which there is social agreement as society necessitates some
agreement, those for which there is no recognised rational justification and on which agreement is not necessary. In seeking rational
autonomy, moral education must view these levels differently, treat-
ing the first as having an authority and status that make education
in commitment justifiable, the last having a status that makes education in commitment totally indefensible.

But this is an over-simplification in many respects, two of which
must be commented on. In practice there is at any given time no
clear demarcation between the first two of these levels. That is always
the state of human understanding in any area at a particular time.
That this is so is simply a fact of the situation, and education can only
seek to be as informed as possible in its practice without being swayed
unduly by current fashions in claims about moral rules. Secondly, it
may seem to have been implied that all rationally defensible principles and rules are about matters on which public agreement is
necessary. This is, however, surely not the case. On some matters
which can be regarded as private, there may be clear rational principles. How is moral education to view these? Are people to be so
educated that, on private matters that are morally wrong, their
understanding of that fact and their dispositions, emotions and role
behaviour are ignored? This is rather like asking if, in areas in which

a person's beliefs will have no public consequences, we should concern ourselves with his believing what is true and behaving accordingly. The consequences of ignoring either understanding or action in both cases might well be disastrous for the individual, and for that reason alone an understanding of the issues is surely necessary. It has never been suggested that education should ignore private moral issues simply because they are private; indeed, I have argued just the reverse where the religious aspects of morality are concerned. To the extent that private issues can be rationally approached, it seems to me that both understanding and all other aspects of the moral life are matters for moral education. If education is concerned with the life of reason, it is concerned with that totally, public or private.

EDUCATION AND THE SECULAR SCHOOL

In all this discussion of education I have refrained from any indication of the particular roles of different social institutions. If education itself ought to be conceived in the secularised form I have outlined, in so far as it is education any institution is after, it will be operating within these terms. Because of the very status of religious claims, I have defended the view that all matters of religion should be regarded as private provided that their practices do not contravene rational public morality. This is to defend the rationality of the secular society that is religiously pluralist. In principle, this is the kind of society we have in Great Britain today, even if certain of its particular public moral principles and legal rules need critical scrutiny. In such a society it would be perfectly consistent for maintained schools to engage in secular education as I have characterised it, including moral education. But further, I would argue that in a secular society the schools financed by that society ought to be secular. In so far as they are, they will be involved in giving what I have called secular religious education. They will, however, stop there where religion is concerned. For schools to see themselves as in any way Christian institutions, or Humanist institutions, or any other sort of institution taking up a position on religious matters, is, I think, for them to become involved in activities which are not educational, becoming partisan on matters that society rightly regards as private. I have argued that the notion that schools, or indeed teachers, must be involved in taking a religious position because they are involved in education in matters which demand that, rests on a mistaken denial of the autonomy of educational pursuits. Not only is there no necessity for an educational institution to take a religious position, it is necessary to education that no religious position be embraced. If therefore an institution is established to educate, it will mitigate against that pursuit if it is also involved in religious affairs of a non-educational character. It therefore seems to be both unnecessary that maintained schools should have any particular religious association and thoroughly undesirable for them to be so associated.

Within the secular society which is religiously pluralist, the churches and other religious instituions have a 'private' function concerned primarily with the practice and propagation of various faiths. Neither this practice nor this propagation is primarily a matter of education in the secular sense, though these activities may have certain elements in common with education. The difference between education and these other pursuits may be blurred in the activities of any institution which endeavours to do both, yet that difference is of vital importance, not only for religious education but for moral education too. Where the distinction is blurred, the limits of reason become lost. What is not rationally defensible can appear to have that defence, what is merely the consequence of particular debatable beliefs can be considered a universal, indeed an absolute, truth. Equally, what is rationally defensible may come to be seen as having no such base, but to be merely dependent on highly debatable pronouncements. That the activities of religious institutions may properly be conducted to complement and harmonise with education, rather than run counter to it, is perfectly true. How far religious institutions, because their ends are not those of education, are in fact in harmony with education is another matter. How far they are in harmony with secular religious education in particular is peculiarly important. Worship, preaching and evangelisation are not incompatible with the aims of religious education, but they certainly cannot be part of it.

If institutions are established, as in the case of church schools, at least in part for bringing up pupils in the practice of a faith and, indeed, for the propagation of that faith amongst the young, they are to that extent engaged in something quite other than education, including religious education. That parents might want for their children both this religious involvement and education is perfectly reasonable. I can imagine schools that carry out both functions with care and integrity so that pupils recognise their difference. What happens all too often, however, is that pupils are religiously exhorted but not religiously educated. As far as morality is concerned, it is presented in a setting that is not necessary to it, so that, in both understanding and practice, confusion results. In our developing understanding of the term, the business of the churches is not education. The latter is the right of all and suitable for all, irrespective of personal or parental religious beliefs. If it is to retain that secular and open character, it is surely best conducted in a secular and open institution devoted simply to that task.

If education needs to be distinguished from the central activities of the church, yet more does it need to be distinguished from many activities of the family. Not that much that is educational does not go on in at least some families. Early education must go on there. The problem is again that much else goes on that is different in character and is not to be confused with education. The point or purpose of many family activities is not educational, and the particularity of them, and the attitudes and sentiments involved, are such that, though compatible with education, they are not what education is about. As in the case of religion, they involve particular 'private' beliefs and styles of life on which education is of necessity open-ended and most explicitly so. This is not to criticise the nature of family life. The diversity and richness of human society owes much to it, indeed it makes possible activities and experiences that, like those associated with the church, are amongst the most valued amongst men. But there is a place for undistracted attention to what reason alone can determine. If, as I have argued, that is what education is about, and it has the justification for which I have contended, then institutions to focus exclusively on it surely have a point. A rational society will, of course, have its families and no doubt its churches, but it will also, I trust, have its thoroughly secular schools.[4]

References

1   I am grateful to the editors of *Learning for Living* (March 1972) and *Faith and Thought* (Volume 99, Number 1) for permission to reprint here certain sections of an article, 'Christian Education: A Contradiction in Terms?', printed in both journals.

2   For further comments, see:
HIRST, P. H. (1974). 'Morals, Religion and the Maintained School'. In Hirst, P. H., *Knowledge and the Curriculum*. London: Routledge and Kegan Paul.

3   HIRST, P. H. (1974). *Knowledge and the Curriculum*. London: Routledge and Kegan Paul.

4   For further comments, see HIRST, P. H. (1967). 'Public and Private Values and Religious Educational Content'. In Sizer, T. R. (ed.), *Religion and Public Education*. Boston, Mass.: Houghton Mifflin.

CHAPTER 6

The Secular Approach to Moral Education

THE AIMS OF MORAL EDUCATION

The various aspects of the moral life of the rational autonomous man that I have characterised express the kinds of achievements with which moral education is concerned. Summarily expressed in a loose phenomenological categorisation, they are as follows:

A   (i) Procedural knowledge or 'know-how' of the logic of rational moral judgments.

    (ii) Procedural knowledge of social skills and roles.

B   (i) Propositional knowledge or 'know-that' of the fundamental moral principles.

    (ii) Propositional knowledge of the physical world.

   (iii) Propositional knowledge of persons, both self and others.

   (iv) Propositional knowledge of social institutions and roles.

C   (i) Dispositions, conscious and unconscious, to think and judge morally.

    (ii) Dispositions, conscious and unconscious, to act in accordance with moral judgments.

D Emotional experiences in keeping with rational moral judgments which facilitate moral action.

This categorisation of kinds of achievement is of elements which are interrelated both within and across these categories in many complex ways. The categories could of course also be subdivided to provide much greater specificity, by expanding, for instance, the kinds of know-how needed in A(i) in terms of the logical rules involved and the processes of thought demanded, or the types of knowledge of persons needed in B(iii) in terms of their emotions, dispositions, beliefs and so on. It must be remembered too that the extent of any individual's achievements within this framework has itself to be rationally considered, for autonomy of this form can only be a matter of degree. Nevertheless, certain achievements across all four major domains would seem essential if autonomy is in fact to exist at all.

Any scheme of this sort is necessarily to some extent arbitrary, and it may be of interest to some to compare it in outline with the more detailed scheme set out by John Wilson[1]. His mapping shows certain different emphases and its rationale, even in its most recent form, is not too easy to grasp. As it was originally constructed to distinguish elements in the moral life of a rational autonomous person as Mr Wilson understands that, it included in its structure particular attention to the elements in a concern for other persons as equals. He has also not sought in his major categories to distinguish throughout phenomenologically, and from this point of view his largest categories overlap. With his way of outlining the elements in more detail I would not disagree to any significant extent and to much that he has written on this subject I am greatly indebted. His outline of distinct areas in which research and assessment into morality are needed will no doubt prove of immense value in helping us to understand both the nature of the moral life and how best to educate for it.[2]

For the purposes of planning moral education, however, we need to know much more than a map of the kinds of achievements we are seeking in the end. Not only must we be more specific about the precise achievements, we must also have some thorough understanding of how these ends can be reached. Unfortunately, on this front we as yet know precious little. The studies that are needed are, in the first place, logical analyses of the various achievements so as to be clear about their necessary prerequisites. If we can distinguish these, then we know something of the limits on developmental processes. In addition, however, we need a great deal of empirical research of a psychological and sociological kind to get at the various factors we must control if learning in all the necessary but diverse areas is to be effective. Right now we are only just beginning to have the philosophical analyses required. The characterisation of the types of achievements involved I have to some extent discussed, of their presuppositions we have only hazy glimpses. Empirical research likewise has as yet provided little on which we can build positively. This is not the place, nor am I the person, to discuss the work of psychologists and sociologists that is relevant. From a philosophical point of view there is, however, a little that can be contributed to our understanding of development, and to that I shall now turn.

Central to the points I wish to make is a notion that has been expressed repeatedly, that the cognitive, intellectual life of a person constitutes a core round which other aspects of his life are organised. That intellectual life itself involves dispositions to think in certain ways. The activity of thinking itself has an emotional tone or significance for the individual. It involves judgments of facts about situations and actions, and whatever the basis of those judgments may be, they form the grounds of all our determinate actions. Again, those judgments of fact and action determine the character of our emotional life. A person's cognitive life is therefore centrally significant for every aspect of his experience. In so far then as we wish a person to develop as a rational autonomous being, the development of this central cognitive aspect of moral life is of prime importance. If we can achieve the appropriate cognitive developments, we will have thereby achieved at least part of what is necessary for other aspects of the moral life. What else is necessary for the dispositional and emotional developments is an immensely difficult problem, but if we could get clear what the achievement of cognitive autonomy presupposes we might be well on our way to finding out the rest.[3]

THE DEVELOPMENT OF MORAL JUDGMENT

Just this has been the interest of a number of distinguished philosophically-minded psychologists who have sought to disentangle the different types of judgment about actions that both children and adults make. Two of these thinkers in particular, Piaget and Kohlberg, have examined with care questions of the stages of development through which children's judgments seem to pass, and have endeavoured to discover how necessary a particular sequence of development might be.[4] Kohlberg's work is the most recent and sophisticated in this area and his conclusions, if they can be sustained, could turn out to be of the greatest educational significance. By putting to children and others in several very different societies a number of moral dilemmas and analysing their responses, he argues that these reveal three distinct levels, each subdivisible, making six stages in all, to which types of moral judgments belong. These stages constitute a sequence through which an individual's judgments can progress, which is invariable and which is universal for all cultures.

Though the particular moral rules in societies may differ radically, the types of judgment made by members of these societies are identical in their formal features. The members of some societies may not in general have reached the later stages of this sequence, and even in societies where many members have reached a later stage, others may be at earlier points of development. In a society like our own, in which many adults operate at the last stage, adults can be found at all the earlier stages and children and young people can be seen at all the different levels. The reason why these stages are found to be invariable and universal, though the terminal points of individuals and societies may differ, Kohlberg claims, is that they demand formal concepts and patterns of reasoning that are in a logical order. The concepts and patterns in stage 5 presuppose those of stage 4, which in turn presuppose those of stage 3 and so on. Thought of the character of stage 5 is thus unintelligible without prior mastery of thought at stage 4. Just as one could not know what a mermaid is unless one knows what a fish is and a girl is, so one cannot judge what ought to be done, in the rational, autonomous way I have considered, without previously knowing how to judge by reference to a set of independently-given rules. These stages are thus in the end distinguishable by philosophical analysis as being in a logical order to which development towards later stages must conform.

The sequence of levels Kohlberg sets out is briefly as follows. In the first, preconventional level, the emphasis is egocentric; good and bad, right and wrong, are labels fixed to actions because of the pleasure or pain, punishment or reward they bring. Deference to power is right just because of its consequences to the individual and any element of justice is simply a question of 'you be nice to me and I will be nice to you'. At the second, conventional level, right and wrong are determined according to rules laid down beyond oneself. Regardless of consequences to oneself, the rules of one's family, school, or nation, and their maintenance, is the basis of judgment. What is approved by these others, what is their will, following their rules as binding, is the essence of the judgment. Authority, in the maintenance of an impersonal social order for its own sake, is what matters. The final level of autonomy is where the question of the validity of rules and values is raised, and right and wrong become judged independently of even one's own groups. At the lower of the two stages within this level, stage 5 in the over-all structure, there is an awareness that there are differences of opinion and that where agreement is necessary there must be a method for reaching a consensus which can later be reconsidered. Agreement and contract are fundamental notions. At the final stage, right and wrong are defined by self-chosen principles of a universal, comprehensive and consistent character concerned with justice, equality and respect for persons.

For reasons similar to those I have given earlier, Kohlberg sees his stages as marking out, not only the sequence of development in moral judgments, but also that in the development of morally significant emotions, and in related dispositions of thought. The quality of affective life differs at the different levels, being determined by cognitive elements, and such feelings as those of fear and guilt must thus be seen as going through a developmental sequence parallel to that of moral judgments. If one adds to this that Kohlberg also claims that there is a close relationship between more developed moral judgment and the actual actions carried out, the sequential story begins to look like providing a framework for moral development as a whole. Clearly, the last of the six stages in this sequence is marked by features I argued to be at least part of the rational autonomous life, and if that is, as I also argued, the aim of moral education, this framework of development provides a framework for moral education too. Granted that, we next need to know how indeed the successive patterns of judgment can be achieved at each stage.

Kohlberg's answer is not easy to express. People do not, he maintains, come to a new form of understanding and judging a situation simply because there are others around who express judgments of that kind or act on judgments different from our own. Ways of judging are not simply internalised when presented to one in some form or other. They are not therefore learnt in the ordinary way in which we imagine people take up, say, the information we give them. Cognitive change, of the type we are concerned with, can occur only by social participation and role-taking of appropriate types. Each stage involves different ways of taking the role of others, both reacting to them as like oneself and reacting to one's own behaviour from their point of view. At each stage there are certain rules for the situation, there is some form of concern for others and there is some concept of justice. All these features are modified as development takes place from one stage to another. What promotes the advancement of a person's thinking from one stage to the next is the result of an awareness of conflicts that arise by seeing the situation in the limited terms of the existing stage of thought. What is crucial for development then is a social context in which conflicts arise for the individual and appropriate role-taking is possible. It is in the stimulation or provoking of the restructuring of how people understand situations that we can promote moral development. One important point about this, that is indeed a consequence of the logical order of the stages, is that children can only adapt to changes that are demanded by the very next stage above and not by stages beyond that. To provoke a consideration of the situation in terms of the roles two stages ahead achieves nothing. What matters in moral education, then, is that in the family, in the peer group, in school, and indeed in wider society, children and young people are stimulated to participate in activities and thought relevant to their present experience and context, that will induce conflicts resolved by a cognitive shift into a new mode of judgment. It is the pupil's active involvement in these considerations that alone is effective.

What the complex mechanisms are within this form of development is not yet clear. At each stage, the preconditions for conflict to arise are very varied. There are demands in terms of the knowledge of the world, of other persons, of society that are vital to forms of role-taking. There is the place of language in capacities to generalise and in promoting an awareness of conflict in one's own and others' roles. Our social institutions may indeed need thorough review if they are not to involve people in roles and thought that are inappropriate, either to the moral development they have achieved or in terms of that which we are seeking to promote. In general terms, however, there would undoubtedly seem to be much of very real importance. It is certainly true that, if children are ever to be rationally autonomous in morality as in anything else, they can only become so by the acquisition of the necessary concepts and that in its turn demands two things: that they acquire these concepts in the proper logical relations, and that they develop them in a context in which they understand how the concepts apply. If these two things are put together they must engender a sequence of development of the Kohlberg kind. To treat young children at stage 1 as if they were capable of judgments about actions at stage 4 is irresponsible, being a logical and educational nonsense. It will promote nothing of value, if it does not do a great deal of harm. To pretend that children can acquire that concept of moral rules that autonomous adults have without having first come to understand what living by rules that are not egocentrically determined involves, is an equal nonsense. To imagine that a stage of moral life in which adults determine for children appropriate rules can be by-passed is to undermine the children's development towards autonomy. In dealing with any given group of children we have also to recognise that, though many pupils may have progressed through to higher stages of development, others may not have done so. Even for those who have progressed, the earlier stages of thought are not totally lost. Not only do we all regress at times, but concerns for, say, reward, or external authority, do not cease to figure in our judgments. Any society or group is therefore complex in its character and so is even the most morally developed person. No one concerned with moral education can therefore ever responsibly ignore the differences in individual development, the significance for them of differences in the institutions those individuals meet, and the complexity of their responses to them.

THE WIDER PROBLEMS OF MORAL DEVELOPMENT

Yet there are many reasons for thinking that Kohlberg's approach cannot tell us the whole of the story of moral development, even when its details are worked out.[5] The very form of the dilemmas Kohlberg put to his subjects determines to some extent the view of morality they express. There are complexities too in distinguishing, in the replies obtained from subjects, such differences as that between what they do actually think and what they judge questioners expect them to think. Or again, between conclusive reasons for judgments and reasons that are simply relevant considerations. What exactly is going on in the mind of the subject when he responds is highly relevant to the significance of research findings and this is far from clear. Another crucial consideration is that, though Kohlberg regards his stages as mapping out a logical sequence, he has not demonstrated in any careful logical analysis that this is the case. His results are based on empirical investigation, and logical relations are not verifiable in this way, even if one may be alerted to them by empirical evidence.[6]

His work does, of course, concern itself only with the formal features of moral reasoning and the concepts that reasoning requires. But that a significant body of substantial moral principles can be rationally justified, using the very form of autonomous reasoning he sees at the last stage, is not a consideration he takes up. The outcome of forms of reasoning is not his concern. Yet this outcome is in a very real sense what morality is all about. It is conclusions in judgment we are after. True, consciously deliberated rational and autonomous judgment will provide the right conclusions, but most of our judgments cannot be so made. Either because of our ignorance, or because of the immediacy of life, social life has of necessity to be conducted on some substantive rules and principles. Again, many people are not capable of autonomous judgments; they are therefore dependent on a body of substantive conclusions. It is also the case that the very social situations Kohlberg sees as critical in moral education presuppose substantive moral rules of some kind, both logically and as providing a context for suitable role-taking to occur. For these reasons, whilst seeking maximum appropriate autonomy, education is to my mind thoroughly justified in working within a framework in which behaviour, habits and dispositions are promoted that conform to the most defensible body of substantive conclusions we have got. This is not to say that we should not be much more careful than we are at present about the particular rules and principles we work on, for many things parents and teachers insist on are not in fact rationally defensible. Nor is it to deny for one moment the necessity for allowing pupils at each stage of development to exercise their role-taking capacities, accepting their need to do so as one important principle in our dealings with them. But wherever the provision of principles and rules is itself rationally defensible, I see no grounds for pretending that reason does not give us an important body of rules and principles. Some of these are so related to man's basic characteristics that they are pretty well universal for all reasoning men, some are necessary to our society's functioning as it is, and some are tentatively defensible. All of these are always up for questioning, but right now they are the best we have and to deny that is to contradict the very concern for reason on which this whole approach is based.

This emphasis on the place in education of particular moral rules and principles suggests that Kohlberg's approach to the development of moral judgment cannot provide a total account of what moral education must involve. Within his account he gives the impression that the development of both dispositions to judge morally and the affective aspects of the moral life, because they are logically related to levels of cognitive development, will almost look after themselves. But if cognitive development is necessary to these other forms, it is far from clear that it is sufficient for them. What else is needed we simply do not know in any detail. Again, that behaviour and cognitive judgment are highly correlated he regards as fortunate, and that is surely true. But we need to know much more about their relationship, for we all know of the gaps between thought and both action in moral matters and dispositions to behave. These are immensely important to the moral life, especially in contexts where immediate action is required. If moral concepts are learnt as concerned with judgments that are binding on action, then they are learnt in a context of developing dispositions to act, but the judgment still does not necessarily result in the action and we need to find out much more of the psychological link.

If, then, we can elucidate the learning that Kohlberg's developmental account itself presupposes and demands, and look at the other forms of learning of non-cognitive kinds that his cognitive story deals with inadequately, there seems to be a considerable place in moral education for types of learning that psychologists and sociologists with very different points of view have examined. There is here little that can at present be said from a philosophical angle that might be helpful in elucidating these areas of moral education. Unlike Kohlberg's theory, which is related to philosophical work on the nature of judgments and their logical relations, the nature of dispositions and emotions is philosophically so unclear that no equivalent attempt to understand their development exists.[7] The empirical findings in psychology and sociology that are of interest for moral education consist largely of correlations between many different aspects of moral life and other personal and social characteristics. There have been many studies on, for instance, altruism, resistance to temptation, aggression, delinquency, patterns of ideals and their correlation with, for example, age, sex, intelligence, social class, and many different character traits. These studies have so far not resulted in any clear picture of the learning processes that take place. Learning theorists have sought to account for moral behaviour and its dispositions largely in terms of complex forms of conditioning by punishment and reward. Parents, teachers, and indeed social institutions and roles, shape people's behaviour by, for instance, physical punishment, stopping things they like to do and withdrawing affection on the one hand, and by praise, financial inducement and access to power on the other. By appropriate patterning of these responses, not only can behaviour itself be shaped, but also a person's own monitoring in terms of such feelings as anxiety can be related to forms of behaviour. There are many general principles involved in such an approach, derived from animal and child studies, but most of these demand forms of control over learning that are not readily accessible in education, and their operation is as yet so inadequately related to other forms of development in education, and that of autonomy in particular, that their proper significance has yet to be made clear.

A similar problem of assessing proper significance in education exists over the interesting results of psychoanalytic studies. Central to their account is the internalisation of control over actions. In complex ways connected with parental relationships, very young children introject aspects of others and develop a super-ego that acts as if it were those others. There is a basic mechanism of identification which seems to operate so as to establish both a form of self-punishment in a sense of guilt and an ideal self. Fully worked out, this is a very sophisticated theory of moral development. It is, however, not only highly disputed, but in important respects untestable, every outcome to investigations being compatible with the theory, 'heads I win, tails you lose'. Even if substantiated, as a basis for educational proposals it at present seems to suffer, like other theories, from a lack of applicability in educational contexts and a lack of adequate relationship to the other significant concerns of education. But this is not the place, nor am I the person, to comment further on empirical research into moral behaviour and moral learning. The results of recent work can be found elsewhere. These asides on emprical matters have been made only to stress the need for research that is developed in a framework in which educationally significant questions can be faced. For all its limitations as yet, Kohlberg's empirical research is based on such a framework and is philosophically informed. In other areas the framework itself hardly exists, maybe because the philosophical work necessary yet remains to be done. There are, however, interesting signs that in both psychology and sociology there is a new interest in the philosophical features implicit in empirical research, and it is to be hoped that these will lead to work that will have more impact on educational practice.[8]

Right now there are very severe limits to the positive suggestions for the practical conduct of moral education that can be confidently expressed on the basis of well-founded research. The over-all aims of such education can now be discussed in a reasonably clear-headed way, though only recently has that become possible.[9] When it comes to the processes of moral education, there is little more we can do at present other than try to harness the most successful processes we have to appropriate aims in as coherent a way as possible. That means building on the most informed and considered experience, keeping in mind what we do know from relevant philosophical and empirical research. But then perhaps this is what all responsible educational development does even when most sustained investigation of the issues has been carried out. Certainly, it is from this limited point of view only that the practical suggestions for moral education in schools are made in the next chapter. Nothing that is there expressed is in any sense tightly deduced from what has been discussed in earlier chapters. The suggestions are merely indications of lines of practice which it is hoped are not inconsistent with what has gone before and which are perhaps at least worth serious consideration.

References

1 For a recent summary, see:
   WILSON, J. (1972). *Practical Methods of Moral Education*. London: Heinemann. Part I and Appendix.
   For a much fuller outline, see:
   WILSON, J. (1973). *The Assessment of Morality*. Slough: N.F.E.R.
2 WILSON, J. (1973). *The Assessment of Morality*. Slough: N.F.E.R.
3 For a most illuminating account of moral development and the moral life that starts from this point of view, see PETERS, R. S. (1973). *Reason and Compassion*. London: Routledge and Kegan Paul.
4 See PIAGET, J. (1932). *The Moral Judgment of the Child*. London: Routledge and Kegan Paul.
   KOHLBERG, L. (1971). 'Stages of Moral Development'. In Beck, C. M., Crittenden, B. S., Sullivan, E. V. (eds), *Moral Education*. Toronto: University of Toronto Press.
5 See WILSON, J. (1973). *The Assessment of Morality*. Slough: N.F.E.R. Chapter 2.
   PETERS, R. S. (1973). *Reason and Compassion*. London: Routledge and Kegan Paul. Lecture 1.
6 There are interesting comments on the development of moral concepts in RAWLS, J. (1972). *A Theory of Justice*. Oxford: Clarendon Press.
7 WILSON, J. (1973). *The Assessment of Morality*. Slough: N.F.E.R.
   WILSON, J. (1972). *Philosophy and Educational Research*. Slough: N.F.E.R.
8 HARRE, R. and SECORD, P. F. (1972). *The Explanation of Social Behaviour*. Oxford: Blackwell.
   FILMER, P., PHILLIPSON, M., SILVERMAN, D., WALSH, D. (1972). *New Directions in Sociological Theory*. London: Collier-Macmillan.
9 The writings of R. S. Peters and J. Wilson are largely responsible for this development, though they have been working in the context of recent developments in moral philosophy associated particularly with R. M. Hare and K. Baier.

CHAPTER 7

Moral Education in the Secular School

I have argued that a secularised approach to the moral life must be welcomed by all rational men, Christians included, and that such a moral life must be characterised by rational autonomy. I have argued for the secularisation of education and for the place of the secular school in our secular society. I have outlined too the general aims of moral education and have commented on the severe limitations of our knowledge as to how best to do the job. But what can be said of the demands for moral education on the secular school in particular? To that I must turn in conclusion.[1]

THE MORAL CHARACTER OF THE SCHOOL

First, I think we must recognise the precise significance of the school in this context. Moral education necessarily begins with the family and to some extent may involve other institutions before children ever come to school. Once at school, children are subject to its systematic influence, and though that influence may not be as strong as that of the family, nor even as strong as that of other groups to which the child may voluntarily belong (for example, the Girl Guide movement, or a local youth club), its persistent educative and socialising effects are important. For many children it is the only source of regular moral influence they encounter, apart from that of their home and their peer group. We must recognise too that the home is on many moral issues severely limited in its approach. Kohlberg has suggested that some 75 per cent of American adults never get to the last of his six stages of moral development. If that is so, then very many homes in the States, and no doubt in Britain too, can offer little of direct help in promoting the later stages I have argued are essential to truly moral development. In such a situation the school must obviously take seriously the job of moral education, doing all of a positive kind it possibly can. Not that it could ever evade involvement in moral matters, for by the nature of the case it is an institution that has social rules and roles which must embody moral principles of some sort, and as an educational institution it is involved in much explicit and implicit teaching and training that bear on all the aspects of the moral life instanced earlier.

In getting clear its role, however, the school must not, of course, ignore the preceding education children have received at home, the influence of the home and other institutions and groups whilst they are at school, or the nature of the wider society into which pupils will move as adults. With very young children, the school must at first act as an extension of the family; to use a well-worn phrase, it is *in loco parentis*. But it is important to recognise from the start that the school is a very particular type of community. To accept that it is not, and cannot be, a family is at least a step towards finding its distinctive educational contribution. In matters of general protection and welfare during school hours, the school must, of course, always be *in loco parentis* and the law rightly demands this. Equally, where a suitable home background is temporarily or permanently missing the school may well have to take on certain parental roles. Yet this notion of a family function inappropriately expresses the moral education the school as such should carry out. What is distinctive of the school as we know it is that it is deliberately organised for educational ends, it is a public institution that must be based on publicly accepted principles, and it is of a size that permits only certain types of personal relationships. For these reasons, the school has often been seen as in some senses standing between the personalised institution of the family on the one hand and the larger impersonal institutions of adult society.

If this view is accepted, and it seems to me in many respects indisputable, there are a number of aspects of the school that are highly important for our purpose. To begin with, there is the simple fact that, quite apart from its specific educational functions, the life of the school should in all respects be morally acceptable. In the relations between children, between children and adults, between the head of the school and the staff, there should be patterns of behaviour that are justifiable in general terms. Bullying, dishonesty, decisions based on personal convenience, the pointless maintenance of tradition, the irrelevant use of status, all these are indefensible in any institution, and certainly in one which is expressly concerned with moral affairs. If those running the school do not maintain a morally justifiable institution, why should pupils take seriously their explicit moral posturings? But unfortunately a mismanaged school is not only an immoral place in itself, it is implicitly developing in pupils beliefs and dispositions that are highly mis-educative. A bad school is for moral education a powerful negative force, not simply one which produces nothing of positive value.

Looked at this way alone, the general conduct of our schools, even where they are running peacefully and smoothly, often leaves much to be desired. Why this should be so is not difficult to see, though that in no way justifies the situation. The institution is usually asked to carry out a considerable exercise in maintaining a high level of social control of large numbers of young people within a relatively re-stricted space. Where older pupils are concerned, it often has to do this whilst trying to involve them in activities they do not value and in which they have known repeated failure. Again, the very teaching function of the school brings about a strongly hierarchical structure. The teachers are older, presumably have been well educated, and are appointed because on all relevant matters of education they are considered to know whereas the immature pupils do not. Society expects its schools to produce young people who will recognise their own immaturity, respect authority, and abide by existing codes of public morality. In this area, as in so many others, education of the 'primitive' kind is expected, not education to produce rational autonomous people who are trained to criticise their society and to expect a rational defence at every turn. In this situation, the direct exercise of authority in a hierarchical system is almost inevitable. That where the general running of the school is concerned even the academic staff should behave as rational autonomous beings, rather than as the obedient servants of the head, is still not common enough. That pupils of sixteen should be allowed critically to assess and seek to change the rules of the institution that considerably affects their daily lives is still commonly regarded as unthinkable. Such a state of affairs breeds indefensible practices only too readily. From these comments it must not be assumed that I am advocating an extreme form of progressive permissiveness in schools. That would to my mind be equally inappropriate, and it would not produce the moral com-munity I am concerned that the school should be. If a general pat-tern of moral living can be established which is in itself rationally defensible for all the members of the institution, genuinely reflecting their varied levels of moral maturity, that would be something.

THE SCHOOL COMMUNITY AND MORAL EDUCATION

But if Kohlberg and many others are right, even in their most general claims, moral education itself demands that for most people there must be an effective exercise of external authority until well into their teens. The school must therefore express a clear control structure that in both content and manner of exercise is rationally defensible and appropriate for moral learning. The content must, of course, be based on the rational principles I have argued for, articulating a concern for justice, freedom, truth, consideration of interests and respect for persons in ways appropriate in the context. The procedure for formulating and revising these rules, in the light of experience and changes of context, must surely be one that will maximise the reasonableness of the conclusions and minimise the significance of personal power, unjustifiable tradition, and other morally irrelevant considerations. What the best machinery is will vary according to circumstances, but if rational control is wanted, it must fully involve in decision-making all those who will have the responsibility for putting the conclusions into practical effect and, at every point where it is indeed reasonable, those who will be subject to such control. In general a reasoned case for the exclusion of staff from such decisions seems hardly possible if one really does care about having rational authority throughout. Nor can there be a blanket case for the total exclusion of pupils. On the contrary, the case for a considerable involvement of senior pupils on many issues relevant to them, and on which they are fully competent to have a reasoned opinion, is extremely strong. For juniors in a secondary school too, involvement on some issues is not unreasonable and may be educationally most valuable. A school council is perhaps not the only way to determine the content of a school's practical rules and principles. Some matters may be best decided by the staff only. Nevertheless, the case for this type of arrangement seems to me overwhelming, granted the view of morality I have defended.[2]

As to the manner of the exercise of authority, it seems essential that it offer pupils opportunity for practical involvement in role-taking that will enable them to experiment in making decisions and living by them, according to their stage of development. Only in this way can pupils possibly form the necessary concepts and related dis-

H

positions to think and to act. From what has been said before, it is clear that moral education cannot be carried out simply by making pupils' behaviour conform by the external imposition of even the best rules through punishment and reward. Nor is it achieved by their simply being told what to do, nor again by their having teachers as suitable models for behaviour. Their role-taking, in both thought and action, in ways that will promote their understanding, is the crux of the matter. If the system forces them into role-taking of a dependent submissive kind when they should be learning to think in an autonomous fashion, it will only inhibit moral development. Nor, on the other hand, will it do any good to thrust autonomous decisions on pupils incapable of taking them because they have not yet come to recognise the significance of any impersonal rules, let alone of their formulating these for themselves on adequate grounds. What this means is that the over-all framework of authority for the school must at one end of the age range provide firm external control and at the other opportunities for a high degree of autonomy to pupils, yet throughout provide to a maximum areas in which the pupils can reasonably and effectively enter into decisions that actually matter to their life in the place. External authority must therefore be as indirect and as flexible as is reasonable whilst retaining its authority. In particular, the flexibility must be such that pupils can make mistakes of a certain seriousness and consequence for them, provided these are in no major sense ultimately to their harm. And the use of this flexibility in ever more adult and responsible ways must be positively encouraged by teachers, not inhibited. Without this, why should pupils ever reach effective, committed, rational autonomy? Indeed, all the evidence is that they will not. If the school does not produce the right context, autonomy will only come if other agencies provide occasion for it. But perhaps autonomy will then not develop with an appropriate understanding of the significance of reason.

What is here said of the school is, of course, also true of the home, but the very character of the school means that it can promote the appropriate types of role-taking and other elements of learning in a way the home must find difficult.[3] First, the absence of the personal involvement of the family means that early on children can learn to live by impersonal rules and discover the significance of so living, independently of both their own feelings and desires and the protectiveness of their parents. Secondly, the recognition that moral rules are rules not to be justified by personal consideration can readily emerge in this context. The fact that morality is essentially a rational matter, and not one of the private beliefs of a group, is brought out. Thirdly, the size of a school and the varying groupings it permits can offer varieties of opportunity for role-taking that will help to generalise pupils' moral concern to people of diverse abilities, interests, backgrounds, races, creeds and so on. Fourthly, as an institution deliberately concerned with education, it can both plan activities with this role-taking in mind, and it can plan for all the attendant learning of an intellectual kind that is required. Fifthly, because it is an institution only partly open to current social influences, having a protective role for at least some of its pupils and a culturally selective role for all, there is some hope that, if these roles are properly discharged, not only autonomy but rational autonomy might be the outcome.

Yet the limitations for moral education of even an appropriately conducted school are not to be forgotten. The society in which pupils learn their involvement and role-taking is limited in its character. The very fact that schools are protective and culturally selective can mean that they very effectively isolate themselves from highly important aspects of society at large. As institutions they themselves have little or no voice in public life, and they have certainly so far managed, at least in Britain, to keep out any continuing public say in their internal affairs. Indeed, non-involvement in contemporary society and its moral issues, many of which are, of course, tied to matters of political debate, is a mark of school curricula and indeed of schoolteachers. By sheer omission, if nothing else, many schools educate pupils as if social involvement outside their walls were immaterial, a point of view in direct opposition to all that rational autonomy stands for.

Inevitably in this situation schools tend to be inward-looking, to produce role-taking opportunities and involvements that are artificial and not associated with society at large. They can produce, very effectively, in place of a truly moral universalism, principles and rules of living and dispositions that are not only limited in their generalisation, but ill-informed on the attitudes and interests of others and dissociated from the moral issues that really matter in human society. It is therefore important for moral education that we break down the social isolation of the school that seems to follow all too readily from the protective and culturally selective roles it must fulfil. We need to be much more sophisticated in recognising the needs of pupils at different stages of development if they are to become moral beings in any fully rational and autonomous sense.

I have discussed the general organisation and authority structure of schools, but have said little as to how specifically the points I have made can best be implemented. Circumstances must mean differing applications, but unless there are very strong reasons to the contrary in a particular case, the following demands on school organisation seem to me inescapable. First, there must be a firm authority structure whose rules, principles and forms of punishment are clear and defensible. Secondly, it must be one on which pupils of all ages can bring effective influence to bear on all matters on which they are capable of informed judgment. Thirdly, opportunities for the involvement of pupils in the many forms of role-taking, and this means actually assuming the roles, not mere role-playing, that are necessary for their moral development must be found, this in activities not only internal to the school but in relation to moral issues in the community at large. Fourthly, the school needs so to group pupils that it provides a context in which truly moral judgments are encouraged and expressed. If teaching groups are invariably highly setted according to ability, we know only too well that this encourages quite particular morally undesirable attitudes. If such setting there must be for the purpose of academic education, though the arguments in many areas are highly suspect unless traditional patterns of formal class teaching are unreasonably insisted on, then other groupings for activities of real importance to the school are imperative. Fifthly, the school needs to show plainly that it values people as such, that it is indeed moral in its interest in them. Unless there is an institutionalised machinery whereby this interest will be taken in every pupil, it simply will not occur for very many. If teachers meet pupils only in classes where some particular area of academic education is the focus of concern, their understanding of pupils will necessarily be quite inadequate for a relationship in which the complex moral interests of pupils are seriously handled. A tutorial, house or counselling system, in which someone seeks to look at a pupil's experience of school as a whole, trying to help the pupil make sense of it in terms of his life outside school, would seem imperative.[4]

THE CASE FOR EXPLICIT MORAL EDUCATION

Moral education cannot, of course, simply be left to the general influence of the school, even if that includes a properly constituted way in which the individual's interests are fully safeguarded. Adequate education in this area, as in any other which involves a great deal of understanding and intellectual mastery, necessitates much explicit learning. Somewhere, somehow, every school curriculum should provide opportunity for pupils to acquire the very considerable amount of knowledge that is necessary for morally responsible living in our complex democratic society, and the intellectual skills and dispositions the making of moral judgments demands. Where sheer knowledge of facts about the world and society is concerned, it is remarkable how little care we take to make sure that school-leavers are well-informed for the responsibilities they must take on. Whether one is talking about such personal matters as, say, sex and drugs, or civic matters about the law and the working of political institutions, we have still not started to get to grips with producing curricula that are responsibly planned. And that in a situation where society progressively gives young people more and more personal freedom and more and more social and political power. Freedom and power in the hands of people who are simply ignorant of what they are involved in are hardly likely to produce the good life for anyone. In both the natural sciences and social studies we need to map out for all pupils curricula that no longer skirt this issue. We are still addicted to the idea that pupils learn what is important by in fact learning something else. The understanding relevant to teenagers' problems of sex and drugs that actually emerges from biology lessons is often very limited and dangerous in its partiality. The understanding as to how public institutions in our society actually work that emerges from the study of British history, the nearest many get to the matter, is usually minimal. Do we not care that so many schools do nothing to enable pupils to understand the contemporary significance of, say, trade unions, local government, or public finance?

Knowledge of this factual kind is, however, far from adequate for the making of moral judgments in both the personal and public areas of life. An understanding of the attitudes, feelings, values and motives of people is equally important. In school, some of this comes from the direct experience of living with others in the school, but that is necessarily so limited that much more is required. In the study of literature, history and religion there is a great opportunity for pupils to understand 'how people tick', to enter imaginatively into situations of great diversity. It needs to be more widely recognised, however, that this understanding of people is indeed what education is after in these subjects, at least in part. Only too often very little of this kind is sought and even less gained. Maybe, if it is understanding people we want, other media have much to offer: film, drama, TV. And yet more, perhaps we must again go directly for what we want by extending pupils' personal experience, educating them within situations that communicate face to face other attitudes, values and so on. Psychologists have had much to say here about the need for pupils to come to understand themselves, their own feelings, attitudes and values.[5] Achieving a sense of personal identity, as someone who counts in the eyes of others, has a significant role to play in the community, who has enough confidence to express a coherent personal point of view, all this matters greatly. No doubt the life of the school outside curriculum areas is the context in which much of this sense of oneself develops, if only because of the diverse opportunities for experiment and role-taking that are possible. Nevertheless, the curriculum itself can offer considerable scope as well. New activities for achieving personal understanding need to be built into school work and, if many of these are not likely to be highly theoretical in character, there is no doubt a place too for responsible teaching in elementary psychology and sociology.

These critical suggestions inevitably lead to the question as to whether moral education should enter curricula as a distinct subject or area of study. Though much of the understanding I have just been discussing can be catered for within other curriculum units, and to my mind should be so handled, I think there is nevertheless an overwhelming case for bringing together the relevant knowledge in periods concerned explicitly with moral education. Every curriculum area deals with matters related to some moral problems, but most cannot deal very readily with all the different matters relevant to many complex issues without deliberately devoting considerable time to them. If, however, one recognises that learning to make moral judgments involves learning to ask particular kinds of questions and to reason in particular ways, then the case for explicit attention to moral questions in time set aside specially for this work becomes very strong indeed. Not only is it then recognisably one person's responsibility to see that the necessary knowledge is in fact acquired by pupils, it is his responsibility also that they reach an appropriate mastery of the logic of moral discourse and a grasp of fundamental moral principles. The whole question of pupils grasping the significance of public and private morality in society, the relationship between morals and religion, law and convention, all these are matters adequate education must take on at an appropriate time. Periods allocated for this purpose seem to me inevitable. Not that any aspect of moral education should be left to such periods only; if a highly suitable opportunity presents itself for dealing with the matter on some other occasion it should be used. Flexibility is of the essence of good education, but within a recognised scheme of responsibilities. Nor am I suggesting that periods set aside for this work should be labelled 'M.E.' Labels are immaterial as long as they are not misleading, and periods set aside for moral education can readily occur within areas designated by the labels of topics dealt with or under such headings as 'modern society' or 'humanities'. I would, however, myself resist explicit work in moral education being swept up under the label of an existing conventional school subject that would be misleading.

In particular, it seems to me undesirable to deal with moral education under 'English'. That linguistic and literary study has much to contribute to moral education is, of course, true. That conventional syllabuses in this subject can readily include many other elements necessary to moral education I would reject. The pretensions of certain literary critics and teachers of English have done much to confuse, rather than elucidate, the nature of moral issues, and have encouraged many teachers quite unqualified for the job to undertake a dangerously inadequate approach to moral education through the use of English literature.[6] Nor do I think it appropriate that moral education be simply subsumed under 'religious education' or 'religious studies'. Such a procedure, whatever the form of teaching it covers, is of itself liable to suggest that morality is not autonomous, when its autonomy is one of the central elements that needs to be taught. If religious education is being conducted with the aims I have suggested are appropriate for the secular school, an understanding of the relationship between certain religious positions and certain moral beliefs and practices will be included. This involves recognising, however, that moral education is in a very different position from religious education as commitment to certain rational moral principles is thoroughly justifiable. The central concern of the school with moral education should therefore be dissociated from religious education, it being accepted that only by some is morality thought to have a religious relevance and that that relationship is in any case irrelevant to the justification of moral principles.

In insisting on the need for specific attention to moral education in the curriculum, I have tried not to deny the significance of all other areas of the curriculum for this work. Every element of the curriculum will involve pupils in learning forms of thought as well as a content which have their place in moral understanding. All teaching contexts too involve relationships and patterns of behaviour that are significant in learning moral conduct. It is the adequacy of any and all of these contexts for this particular job that I am calling in question. I am suggesting too that no teacher trained in any established academic discipline, and skilled in teaching it, is thereby knowledgeable about either the nature of moral problems and their solution or the best ways of carrying out moral education. What we need are teachers who have studied the nature of morality, who have the necessary contributory forms of understanding on an appropriate area of moral questions, and are trained to teach in this area. There are at present few such people available. That there should be teachers with this specialism is to many a sinister proposal, for must not all members of the profession be morally educated to a degree that would qualify them to do this job, and is one not in danger of producing moral authorities of a dangerous kind? That all teachers are expected to be educated sufficiently to use English in an accurate and appropriate way is not regarded as a reason for denying the necessity for specialist teachers in this area. Most teachers would be quite inadequate in the area, possessing none of the necessary analytical grasp of the subject matter or of its presentation. Much the same must be true where morality is concerned. Nor are moral specialists to be feared if they are indeed aware of the real nature of morality and of the importance of rational autonomy. It is the evangelist, or the 'specialist' who does not understand the nature of the subject matter, who is the menace. But such people are a menace in every area and that fact cannot be allowed, in moral education any more than elsewhere, to cloud the question as to what the proper conduct of the professional task necessarily demands: teachers adequately educated in what they teach and trained to educate others accordingly.

TEACHING MORALITY

If it is agreed that the school curriculum should specifically deal with morality, what precisely should be done in the time available? From an intellectual point of view, there must be a place for developing the many elements of necessary knowledge and understanding that I have referred to repeatedly. This can be done in a great variety of ways and I shall not comment on this further. In particular, of course, there must be attention to moral problems themselves. Which problems at which stage depends on many factors. It is possible to present for discussion, written work, dramatic expression and so on, life situations which are appropriate to the age and interests of pupils. In this way relevant matters of fact and of principle can be harnessed to the making of judgment. New concepts can be developed and new forms of reasoning can be practised, much of this in learning to use and apply moral discourse. But if this is to be effective, Kohlberg's stages must be recognised and the situations provide at least intellectually for the role-taking he insists is crucial. There is, however, every reason to think that if dispositions to think morally are to be developed, the situations and problems used must be of genuine interest to pupils, involve their emotions, their imagination, and their desire to find solutions that would make practical sense for their own actions. It must be the real life of the pupils that is focused on, not the real life of adults.[7] It is also a question of dealing with these, not in detached terms such as 'what ought to be done about racial discrimination in this case?' but rather in terms of 'what ought we to do about this case of racial discrimination we know about?' And that immediately introduces a further point, that if dispositions to act rationally matter as much as dispositions to think rationally, the process of encouraging responsible moral judgments without related action is of itself inadequate and might well encourage an undesirable divorce of moral thought and action. It seems then that at the centre of explicit moral education there should be the study of, and involvement of the pupils in, particular moral activities that they are able to see as important. That means, on the one hand, involving them in the detail of the life of the school community and using that fully as an educational instrument both theoretically and practically. On the other hand, it means involving pupils significantly in moral issues in the society outside the school, again not only theoretically, but in action as well. If both these are done, they will provide opportunity too for the development of social skills without which the moral life can be only too easily vitiated. It is encouraging that there are now becoming available both materials for use in school and suggestions for relevant activities both inside and outside the school that will help just this kind of work.[8]

There is a tendency to think of moral education as simply a matter of the discussion of suitable material, and it must be apparent that that is to my mind, on its own, much too limited an approach. Nevertheless, discussion must be a vital part of the process provided it is seen as a teaching method. The airing by pupils of their ignorance and prejudice whilst a teacher assumes a form of moral neutrality is a travesty of education.[9] The open-ended nature of debate on controversial matters must indeed be recognised when such matters are discussed, but that that is true of all moral issues cannot, on my argument, be held by any rational person. If it is the job of the teacher to promote rational autonomy, discussion is useful as a method only in so far as it promotes that end. Let us by all means have much more discussion work of this kind, but let us have it geared to the development of reason and indeed to the development of rational action. In that case, the method will be characterised neither by an irresponsible acceptance of pupils' autonomy uncontrolled by reason, nor by an uncritical indoctrinatory imposition of the moral opinions of the teacher.[10] In moral education, as in any other area of education, what is asked of the teacher is a total commitment to the development of rational autonomy in both thought and action. Teaching that begins to suggest that any beliefs cannot be rationally called in question, or that seeks to develop dispositions against such questioning, is not acceptable. But to say that is perfectly consistent with also saying that in morals, as in mathematics, history, or any other area, there may be a body of beliefs and principles that can be taught with confidence as having substantial rational defence. It is the job of the professional teacher to know the limits of that defence and to be true to those limits. Where reason can offer no conclusions, education can offer none either. Where reason can offer conclusions, even if they are provisional as in so many matters, to pretend otherwise is unreasonable. What education demands is that in content, teaching methods, discipline and relationships within the school, teachers be governed by nothing but reason.

The central problem in education today seems to be a failure of nerve on just this very point. Not only moral education but education as a whole seems to be losing some of its bearings in moving from a primitive concept to an unqualified concern for reason. Of course, such failure of nerve is understandable when society is undergoing so many changes, when reason has made such mistakes in the past and has proved so powerless against the forces of unreason. No wonder we neither stick consistently to principles and practices for which the rational defence is abundant, nor follow consistently new lines of development where reason manifestly demands them. But this failure of nerve must be overcome if educational, and indeed social, disaster is to be avoided. After all, there is no basis other than reason for meaningful human development. Both personal and social salvation may to the Christian have their source in God, but I see no grounds for thinking that, even on that view, human reason can properly be set on one side. The secular society is supremely the product of reason, God-given reason if you will. Its problems come not from the development of reason, but from our refusal on so many fronts actually to live accordingly. There are today very few major social issues on which the most disruptive elements in our society have not got a highly defensible reasoned case. True, irrational elements may repeatedly take over the cause, but they take over the defence of the *status quo* as well. We do not live in a society that is morally defensible in its distribution of power, wealth, or, for that matter, true education. We deceive ourselves if we think otherwise. The increase of secularisation with its attendant growth of reason has made this plain to a point where it can no longer be hidden. What we shall have to do, if our society is not to become morally degenerate and return to control by force, is re-fashion it so that reason can in fact prevail. To this end, moral education in schools has something to contribute, if alone it is powerless against other social institutions. We need the next generation to be more moral than we are, and that means more committed to reason. I am not altogether without hope, provided we can all, Christians and non-Christians alike, stop seeking irrational solutions to our ills and produce education for rational autonomy. That alone is the form of moral education that can properly serve our secular society.

References

1 There is a now classic discussion of matters raised in this chapter, as well as of many other issues dealt with earlier, in:
   DURKHEIM, E. (1961). *Moral Education*. Glencoe, Ill.: The Free Press.
   See also a recent work which discusses the significance for moral education of available empirical research into aspects of the school:
   SUGARMAN, B. (1973). *The School and Moral Development*. London: Croom Helm.

2 A much more extensive discussion of these issues will be found in:
   UNGOED-THOMAS, J. R. (1972). *Our School*. Harlow: Longman Group for Schools Council.

3 For a fuller treatment of several points made here, see:
   LOUBSER, J. J. (1971). 'The Contribution of Schools to Moral Development'. In Beck, C. M., Crittenden, B. S., Sullivan, E. V. (eds.), *Moral Education*. Toronto: University of Toronto Press.

4 This and many other practical aspects of moral education are discussed in:
   WILSON, J. (1972). *Practical Methods of Moral Education*. London: Heinemann.

5 WILSON, J. (1972). *Practical Methods of Moral Education*. London: Heinemann.

6   The background to much of the advocacy of moral education through literary study is to be found in the writings of F. R. Leavis. See particularly his *Education and the University* (Chatto and Windus, 1948). A critical study of this view of literature and its historical origins is to be found in: WILLIAMS, R. (1961). *Culture and Society*. Harmondsworth: Penguin Books.

7   See MCPHAIL, P., UNGOED-THOMAS, J. R., CHAPMAN, H. (1972). *Moral Education in the Secondary School*. Harlow: Longman Group for Schools Council.

8   See particularly:
MCPHAIL, P. (1972). *In Other People's Shoes*. Harlow: Longman Group for Schools Council. Also materials of the Schools Council Project in Moral Education published under the title *Lifeline*.
(1970). *Schools Council and Nuffield Humanities Project: An Introduction*. Heinemann Educational. Also handbooks and materials developed by the Project. Community Service Volunteers: materials produced under the general direction of Dickson, A.

9   See BAILEY, C. (1973). 'Teaching by Discussion and the Neutral Teacher'; and ELLIOTT, J. (1973). 'Neutrality, Rationality and the Role of the Teacher', both in *Proceedings of the Philosophy of Education Society of Great Britain*, Volume VII, Number 1.

10   The concept of indoctrination has been widely discussed by philosophers. See: SNOOK, I. H. (ed.) 1972. *Concepts of Indoctrination*. London: Routledge and Kegan Paul.

THE NATIONAL CHILDREN'S HOME
CONVOCATION LECTURESHIP

Former lectures in this series are:

1974: 'Moral Education in a Secular Society', by Paul H. Hirst, M.A.; *Professor of Education, University of Cambridge*. Published by University of London Press Ltd., St. Paul's House, Warwick Lane, London EC4P 4AH.

1973: 'Care Can Prevent', by Philip Barker, M.B., M.R.C.P.ED., M.R.C.PSYCH., D.P.M., D.C.H.; *Consultant in Clinical Charge, Charles Burns Clinic, Birmingham; Lecturer and Post-Graduate Clinical Tutor in Child Psychiatry, University of Birmingham; Consultant Psychiatrist to Birmingham Child Guidance Clinic and the National Children's Home.*

1972: 'Recipe for Failure', by Sir Alec Clegg; *Chief Education Officer for the West Riding of Yorkshire.*

1971: 'Planning for Deprived Children', by Roy A. Parker, B.SC. (SOC.), PH.D.; *Professor of Social Administration, University of Bristol.*

1970: 'Leadership in Residential Child Care', by Haydn Davies Jones, B.A., LL.B., LL.M.; *Tutor, Advanced Course in Residential Care and Education of Children, University of Newcastle upon Tyne.*

1969: 'Children and Society a Hundred Years Ago', by Jean S. Heywood, B.A., PH.D.; *Director of Post-Graduate Training in Social Work, University of Manchester.*

1968: 'Patterns of Residential Care for Children', by John Gibbs, O.B.E., M.A., L.H.D.; *Lecturer in Psychology, University of Cardiff.*

1967: 'Why Behave? A Guide to the Understanding of Children's Behaviour', by W. Lumsden Walker, M.D., D.P.H., D.P.M.; *Consultant Child Psychiatrist, Bristol Royal Hospital for Sick Children.*

1966: 'The Involved Man—Action and Reflection in the Life of a Teacher', by Kenneth Barnes; *Headmaster of Wennington School, Wetherby.*

1965: 'The Handicapped Child and His Home', by Mary D. Sheridan, O.B.E., M.A., D.C.H. Revised edition 1973.

1964: 'Thirty-Three Troublesome Children', by D. H. Stott, M.A., PH.D.; *Psychology Department, Glasgow University.*

1963: 'The Religious Needs of Children in Care', by the Rev. H. A. Hamilton, B.A.; *formerly Principal, Westhill Training College, Selly Oak; Chairman, Congregational Union of England and Wales, 1961–62.*

1962: 'Children Not Cases', by Kenneth Brill, O.B.E., LL.B., A.A.P.S.W.; *Children's Officer, County of Devon.*

Index